EVOLVING ON PURPOSE

MINDFUL ANCESTORS PAVING THE WAY FOR FUTURE GENERATIONS

KATIE CAREY   AYLEEN HACOPIAN   CELIA LOUISE

CRYSTAL RASMUSSEN   DEBBIE SQUIZZERO

EMMA JOHNSON   JESSICA VERRILL   KALI J WALTERS

KATI LUDWIG   KARE   KATY BAYNES   KELLY BAYE

LEANNE WAKELING   LIBBA PHILLIPS

LIDIA KULESHNYK   SANDRA JOY LARATONDA

SARAH BRIGID BROWN   SHANDRA NICOLE SHULTZ

TAMMY GOEN   TE ARAHI   TRACEY KISSOON

SOULFUL VALLEY PUBLISHING

To Choosing You 3 Evolving on Purpose!

Shandra "Phoenix" Sholtz

CONTENTS

INTRODUCTION   v
KATIE CAREY

1. AYLEEN HACOPIAN- MS,RD,CN   1
*A NEW WORLD VISION WHERE SCIENCE AND
SPIRITUALITY CREATE A ROMANCE!*

   About the Author   15

2. CELIA LOUISE   17
ACKNOWLEDGING YOUR INSTINCTS

   About the Author   26

3. CRYSTAL RASMUSSEN   27
LIVING YOUR LEGACY

   About the Author   37

4. DEBBIE SQUIZZERO   39
FROM SURVIVING TO THRIVING

   About the Author   51

5. EMMA JOHNSON   53
MAKING THE UNCONSCIOUS CONSCIOUS

   About the Author   60

6. JESSICA VERRILL   61
Evolving Through Consciousness

   About the Author   70

7. KALI J. WALTERS   71
LAST TRAIN OUT, FIRST STEP FORWARD

   About the Author   80

8. KARE   81
LOSING KEN, FINDING KARE

   About the Author   91

9. KATY BAYNES   93
SOUL TO HUMAN COHERENCE

   About the Author   106

10. KELLY BAYE   107
CHALLENGE IS GROWTH

    About the Author   123

11. LEANNE WAKELING   125

About the Author   140

12. LIBBA PHILLIPS ©   142
LISTENING TO HEAVEN

About the Author   154

13. LIDIA KULESHNYK   156
HOW TO HEAL AND BECOME THE CONSCIOUS LEADER OF YOUR LIFE

About the Author   166

14. SANDRA JOY LARATONDA   168
DO YOU DEFINE YOUR MONEY STORY OR DOES YOUR MONEY STORY DEFINE YOU?

About the Author   179

15. SARAH BRIGID BROWN   180
THE DAY THE UNIVERSE PUT ME ON THE RIGHT PATH

About the Author   188

16. SHANDRA NICOLE SHULTZ   190
THE RISE OF THE PHOENIX: MY JOURNEY THROUGH ADDICTION

About the Author   202

17. TAMMY GOEN   204
A SENSITIVE JOURNEY

About the Author   214

18. TE ARAHI "The Guide" & KATI LUDWIG   215
THE WEAVING OF ANCESTRAL WISDOM

About the Author   226

About the Author   227

19. TRACEY KISSOON   228
I HAVE ALWAYS WONDERED WHY THERE IS SUCH A DISTINCTION BETWEEN SCIENCE AND SPIRITUALITY

About the Author   241

20. About the Publisher   242
SOULFUL VALLEY PUBLISHING

INTRODUCTION
THE STORY BEHIND "EVOLVING ON PURPOSE"

KATIE CAREY

I have been called in the middle of the night on this gorgeous bank holiday weekend to my magical desk to write my introductory chapter of my first multi-author book as a publisher.

It's 2:40am, and I've been awake for about half an hour. I peered out through the curtains of my bedroom window, and there she was, the beautiful moon in all her glory, still looking almost full. I climbed back into bed, and then the words started to come to me, and I knew it was time.

So here I am. Ready to let them flow onto the pages of this beautiful notebook. Sitting at my magical desk that I dragged in here in January, which led me to become an international bestselling author. A long-held dream that I had been putting off for many years.

How I got here is quite a story. The COVID pandemic had propelled us into a worldwide experience of trauma in March 2020 — it felt bizarre. I had been hearing that we may go into a lockdown (with no clue what that meant). Two weeks before the UK went into lockdown, I was already isolating. My youngest granddaughter was due to arrive in this world, and I was going to babysit for my eldest granddaughter.

It was hugely important to me that I didn't carry anything over to my beautiful family and I felt blessed that I would get to see my new granddaughter on the day that she was born, just three days before we went into a lockdown in the UK.

Had I known how long it would be before I would see them all again, I would have stayed longer. But I got to hold her when they brought her home that evening, and then I went home.

During the lockdown, my divorce papers arrived for me to sign. My ex was sober again. When he was sober, I could see the man I fell in love with. So, I was hesitant, but that sobriety didn't last. In June, he was back to drinking, and finally, I signed the divorce papers and put them in the post box.

A few weeks before, on the 4th of April, I attended an online "444 Angel workshop" with Joanna Hunter and, in May, a five-day podcast challenge with Anna Parker Naples. It was a while before I did anything about it, but I felt so called to create a podcast. It was something I really desired to do, especially with all the contacts I had made over the last couple of years with my own healing journey. I knew that a podcast could help many people.

Once I had closed the door on my toxic marriage, it was time to get on with my own life and my dreams.

The business I had been building was hit with zero sales coming in because of COVID, and I opted for a mortgage holiday. Then I closed my travel business (that I had literally just started). No one was spending on the online coaching events I had been setting up either —no income was coming in.

Joanna was holding a free five-day challenge, all about the elements and how they are connected to your business. It led to me joining her "Divine planning abundant profits course" and I knew that this course was the one to help me if anything was going to change in my business. I signed up for 10 months of payments, which logically I could not afford, but I had now come to a place where I knew and trusted. I decided that the mortgage payments that should have been coming out would cover the cost of this course monthly. There were a couple of hurdles along the way, including bounced payments, that brought up my money wounds, but I finally made the last payment of that course last week. I managed to attend three more of her programmes. During that course, was where my evolution really began to skyrocket. I asked her, on one of her energy clinics, when she said to focus on one thing (because of my health and disabilities), what should I focus on? I knew that I had previously had too many things going on and felt scattered. She suggested that I focus on the podcast. So I did. I felt a real passion for this project. eBay sales began to trickle in again, and I joined Joanna's Younity course, which led me to write a song straight out of a meditation that I went on to use on my podcast. I began focusing on self-love as a priority.

I realised just how out of alignment I had been living. Despite all the alignment tools I was using in my life. With this realisation my boundaries got stronger. I took better care of myself, and another drama with my ex, led to me saying no when he reached out for help again and him moving to Devon over 200 miles away. Of course, the date he moved into his rehab community would be significant. The date that my stillborn elder brother came into the world and departed was the 21st of September. I knew this was another sign—a synchronicity.

In October 2020, I signed up for Joanna's "Lightweb" course. I desired this from the moment I first heard about it. That same week, I was launching the podcast. The Soulfulvalley podcast ranked in iTunes. It was in the new and noteworthy section for a few weeks, and it got to No. 22 in the alternative health category in Britain. No.34 in Ireland and would later reach number 9 in Cyprus and No.21 in the Czech Republic and is now listened to in over 30 countries. Globally ranked in the Top 2% of listened to podcasts. A huge achievement for an unknown podcaster. In the Czech Republic chart, I saw that Lewis Howes was only three spots above me. I was chuffed with this. I love Lewis Howes.

During the Lightweb training, after the first session, I noticed a brown envelope at 9pm on my doormat. Bizarre as I always check the mail. It wasn't there before. It was a letter about my pension. It was very unclear. I just noticed that the monthly payments had gone up a small amount.

I am disabled and had been awarded tier two of my pension to support me. The next morning, I would discover thousands of pounds in my bank account from my pension pot, completely unexpected. I was over the moon. Now I could relax and continue to focus on my inner healing and self-love.

I continued the podcast, getting a yes when I asked Yasmin Boland if she would be a guest. This was huge to me. I've been a Hay House fan for well over a decade and had been following Yasmin for at least a couple of years. I was really taking the full moon and new moon rituals and ceremonies very seriously since COVID began. I went on to train with her as a Moonologist, gaining a certification on the 31st of December 2020. The same day my divorce came through. Another certification to add to the many qualifications, certifications, and skills I've collected over the last decade.

December was busy with the podcast. I had crammed in extra interviews to give myself a break for two weeks. A lady called Brigid popped into my inbox, asking if I would like to write in her multi author book. The deadline was December, just before Christmas. Well, I had the money, but I had paid off a lot of debt, so there wasn't much of it left. The timing wasn't right, so I said no, thank you.

January 2021—I decided to create my vision board. I put a photo on there saying, "Best Selling Author". This was going to be the year I would do it. I could feel it in my bones!

I looked at the desk sitting under my breakfast bar for three years that I had almost sold, as it had been under there blocking the heat from my radiator. I had given up on the dream of writing after I had signed up for a Balboa Press self-publishing package, but because of the chaos going on in my personal life at the time, I didn't go through with it.

I struggled for hours to move my armchair and pull and shove the desk into my living room, but I was determined. I have bone spurs and tears going on in my shoulders with osteoarthritis and fibromyalgia. I live with chronic pain as a regular occurrence, and it's even worse when I overexert myself and exhausting—but there was no one around to help me because no one was allowed to come in again—another lockdown. I just got on and did it. It wasn't long after that when Brigid Holder popped into my inbox again. This time, with a photo of the book cover and the title." Intuitive: Knowing Her Truth". "Katie—I've extended the deadline in my book, are you sure you don't want to write a chapter?" This time, I was excited. I knew—it pulled my heart straight away. I said, yes. It was a couple of days before I heard back after I applied. But my introduction post was on the 13th of January. Of course, the 13th is massively relevant to me. Go and read my chapter in Intuitive: Knowing Her Truth to see why.

Brigid had reached out to me just days after I brought the desk in, and I had just begun the "My million-dollar experiment". This, I knew, was also a step in that experiment—an opportunity for me to invest my way to wealth. I wrote my chapter, and when it was released in March, it went to bestseller in several categories in six countries (I believe—I lost count). The launch had been so exciting. I noticed Brigid talking about her publishing mentor. I joined her workshop, "How to be a six-figure publisher". It was brilliant. I just felt this calling to do it—but I was scared. I had been very focused on my healing journey and didn't want to hustle. So instead, I watched the other ladies who had signed up, and each one of them, created their books and became bestselling publishers and were creating amazing books, with all of their authors becoming bestselling authors. I became an affiliate for a few of them to test whether I could do this. I earned back some of my initial investment to be in the book, which, incidentally, I had earned from affiliating and sharing the million-dollar experiment, with over 60 people joining through me.

I could not stop thinking about the publishing. It felt like this was the bigger picture vision for me. This was how I would learn how to publish my own books and help others to step into becoming an author, the way that I had.

In October, as well as the "Lightweb" course, I signed up for Emma Johnson's "Master Your Money Mind" EFT 16 week course. I knew that consciously my money stories had changed, but my body was still reacting viscerally whenever I noticed a drop in my bank account balance. I knew that to change things, I needed to work on this. The subconscious mind is so powerful. Only 5% of our reality has anything to do with the conscious mind. The subconscious mind makes up 95% of our experienced reality. It's worth learning about. (You will also now find Emma Johnson in this book; she became one of my authors).

Joanna offered another course, "Divine Downloads" in April. I knew this would help with the book titles. I jumped in again, and, at the same time, I also said yes to the Publishing Training. These choices led to me channelling three book titles. I instantly knew which one was the first book. I began advertising that I was launching a publishing house on yet another synchronistic spiritual date for me —the 4th of May. The authors' hub, it turns out I started on the 13th of May. My signs that this was sent to me via spirit.

My first book would be this one, Evolving on Purpose: Mindful ancestors, paving the way for future generations. What a title spirit handed me there. What a magnificent book this could be to serve the world right now as we move forward, thankfully, out of this pandemic.

As you may have noticed, I am forever evolving on purpose and completely invested in my journey because I desire to create a reality that serves me, my family, my community, and makes the changes that I want to see in the world around me.   Self-responsibility is paramount in this new paradigm.   We cannot change the behaviours and actions of others, but we can change ourselves and how we perceive everything, and we can become discerning about who and what we allow into our lives.

I am returning to close this chapter now that all the authors have appeared, and I feel so blessed at the incredible people who have come together from around the world to collaborate with the creation of this book.   Each one arrived in divine timing, with many synchronistic stories about how and why they got here. Together, we have created this awesome book, filled with knowledge and wisdom, that we intend to educate and touch the souls of everyone who reads it. I hope that you enjoy reading this as much as we have enjoyed creating it and that it can help you in your own journey of Evolving on Purpose.

KATIE CAREY
SOULFUL VALLEY PUBLISHING

AYLEEN HACOPIAN- MS,RD,CN
A NEW WORLD VISION WHERE SCIENCE AND SPIRITUALITY CREATE A ROMANCE!

"Evolve your genes intentionally for a higher purpose."

---

*A*ll life and the human body are designed for success, self-healing, and thriving when given the right environment and nourishment suitable to the unique bio-identity of the individual.

Often I speak of "lifestyle habits" which support our well-being, yet I've expanded those habits to encompass what we eat, how we move, think, connect, and the relationship we hold with ourselves and others. The body's great wisdom is interconnected via many organs and biological constituents that carry on biochemical and energetic dialogues with one another in a bi-directional manner. I have been fortunate enough to expand my knowledge through the teachings and wisdom of great educators and guides; a few are mentioned in this chapter. Imagine the time-honored bidirectional body-mind connection that is resilient and thrives when that connection is healthy and vibrant. I am now in unison with you through sharing those teachings to support your growth as we rewrite the "Human Biology Book" together.

Considering the current state of affairs in our society, it feels imperative to attend to this connection. Our mental and physical health should be regarded as the scaffolding on which we built a harmonious life and longevity. How do we maximize our wellness during a global pandemic which has become the attention-grabbing subject of our times? This pandemic has created an environment of challenge which can be all-encompassing. It has presented itself in the domain of our existence both physically and mentally, regardless of our age, race, color, gender, religion, culture, or geographical location. As a result, we now are bringing to light the importance of co-creating a world supported by cooperation, safety, and immunity.

"Nature is based upon cooperation and mutual aid" Gregg Braden

I intend to provide a condensed resource of this complex interplay to help you gain a broader perspective on improving your internal environment through the lens of epigenetics. Epigenetics, the science of gene expression and its perfect counterpart, while nutrigenomics integrates genomic science with nutrition and lifestyle variables.

It is my intention and hope that we utilize the wisdom of our functionally healthy body-mind connection with a new understanding as science has now validated many schools of thought that were outside of the scope of the traditional medical establishment and protocols they deemed to be acceptable. We now know we are achieving results that were formally not practiced and unexplainable at times.

Science has come a long way in understanding whether we have any control over our genes or the environment that resides around them. In biology, and specifically epigenetics and nutrigenomics, the inherited changes in the appearance of gene expression are caused by mechanisms other than changes in the underlying DNA sequence, hence the name epi-Greek: over, above genetics. Bruce

Lipton Ph.D. Cellular Biologist refers to it as the "field" of information surrounding the external of the gene. I often refer to it as the" Soul of the gene!"

Epigenetics and nutrigenomics and their role in the expression of genes have taken great leaps in discovering how the interplay of nature and nurture works. The understanding of experts in the field of Epigenetics in the last two decades has transformed. Health expression is not only gene coding or its environment but also how genes and the environment interact in a perfectly designed environment of your creation.

Dr. Jeffery Bland Ph.D., FACN, FACB shares in *Integrative Medicine: A Clinician's Journal* (IMCJ) about the imprintome.

"Contrary to the ideas of the last several centuries, It's now firmly established that we each contain large cohorts of genes whose state of activation and function is dictated by epigenetic codes. These markings are known to exert pronounced effects on gene transcription and translation and influence lifestyle factors, including diet, behaviors, environment, and social forces." Jeffery Bland

---

Genetic testing has become very popular due to the heightened awareness of disease prevention. The test provides one with the blueprint of possible SNYPs and variations, also referred to as polymorphisms. Polymorphisms may lead to variations in the amino acid sequences-it's makeup of the predisposed, otherwise inherited codes of our genes. Those variations would mean that for the gene to express itself more healthily; it would require specific nutrients that would help the gene express itself through a healthier version, the higher self rather than the unhealthy version, the lower self. In some instances, when two or more of those variations are identified, it would   make   it   imperative   that   a   personalized   lifestyle recommendation would more likely provide the most effective and sustainably functional health outcomes.

Ultimately, it turns out, although we may not have control over what we cannot change, which is our inherited DNA sequence, we certainly have control over what we can change and improve.

"Personalized lifestyle medicine is becoming a reality, thanks to advances like the imprintome that explain the precise manner in which our genes respond to inputs from the outside world like diet." Jeffrey Bland

---

Through this discovery, it would be sensible to say that the gene's environment is highly impacted by the quality of the diet and the availability of amino acids, fatty acids, minerals, and vitamins. This would create the opportunity for the" field" to be impacted by healthy signaling, which in turn helps the cells to be able to express themselves healthily, once again a bi-directional and reciprocal relationship, very much like a beautiful romance.

The following four-step approach introduces the non-genetic factors and a few genetic factors relevant to this chapter that participate in the behavior of the DNA both in the body-biochemical and body-physical.

May the presented framework provide a template that would help further your discovery through the understanding of our fascinating Human body and all of its interconnected systems and thus, by addressing them, provide an experience of beauty, of harmony between your genes and all that it takes to make you uniquely who we are.

1) Discovery and elimination: Remove and Release

The healing process requires reducing body burdens by addressing offending molecules and releasing and eliminating both internal and external toxins. The body's cellular structure, the outer environment, and the physical environment play an essential role in body burden reduction.

This step includes identifying environmental and food toxins, pathogens (bacteria, viruses, parasites), heavy metals, pesticides, environmental pollutants, and allergenic food triggers. These harmful epigenetic influencers are discovered via specific testings, to be released and eliminated properly from the body. Dr. Christopher Shade Ph.D. founder and CEO of Quicksilver Scientific refers to this process of proper elimination as a "push-catch" step during detoxification of harmful toxicants including heavy metals and metalloids.

"One man's food is another man's poison." Hippocrates

Discovering foods, pseudo foods, and neurotoxins that create either intolerance or a full-fledged allergy does not have to be a frustrating process. Gaining knowledge and awareness almost always proves to be beneficial to your overall health. Allergies and intolerances are often overlooked due to the lack of knowledge in identifying the numerous symptoms that they may cause which are not limited to skin rashes, congestion, abdominal discomfort, or difficulty breathing, and also mood, mental acuity, energy, and sleep. The most commonly known allergies and intolerances are caused by, and not limited to, meats from two-legged and four-legged animals, fish and shellfish, milk and products containing dairy, eggs, nuts and peanuts, soy, wheat, histamines, and yeast. Knowing these offenders and eliminating them will decrease the burdens on the body and contribute towards improving our health.

Family genes, medication use, and dietary intake influence the intestinal tract's inner landscape, the microbiome. Due to mentioned factors, the presence of a challenged digestive tract makes room for a state of microbial imbalance, often referred to as dysbiosis. In such a state present with "metabolic offenders," the ingested food will not suffice in providing the body in supporting its metabolic processes, eliminate waste and toxins properly and generate the required energy.

"Often, the statement "You are what you eat" presents itself as a "half-truth." Ayleen Hacopian

---

Thus, understanding the complexity of food consumption and elimination reveals all the remaining steps lied in-between those two processes. You are not just what you eat; you are the expression of what your body recognizes as food, proper digestion, absorption, elimination, and detoxification. Therefore, any hindrance caused by various metabolic and environmental disruptors will determine how well the body's ingested food was recognized and utilized.

Just like foods and nutrients act as molecules of biochemical information, amino acids and peptides act like molecules of emotion. The body receives these organic compounds through food. Every single one of the trillions of cells in the body is naturally composed of amino acids and their "smaller siblings" called peptides. Energy blockages trapped in the physical body and the field surrounding it- above it, often referred to as the aura-energetic field, identified and recognized by physicists is a known phenomenon.

A lifestyle with physical movement that promotes blood flow and heavier breathing helps improve hormones and neurochemistry and contributes to a happier state of being. Daily physical activities assist in the body's ability to buffer stress hormones and release the "energy of the emotion" by motion. Although some may find it much easier to release trapped emotions through physical activity rather than through changing thoughts and mindset, it has been observed that addressing both the body and the mind results in faster and longer-lasting improvements in overall health and vitality when addressing emotional dissonance. The whole style living approach introduced earlier, and its components will require changes in behavior and routines and toxicity-inducing habits propagated by action. There are a variety of complementary therapies to lifestyle therapies to assist in providing homeostasis in the body-mind connection. these include and are not limited to Reiki, light and sound therapy, EMDR, EFT, hypnosis, spiritual healing, bioenergetics, aromatic therapy, energy coaching, ancestral healing, meditation, psychological counseling and talk therapy, and internal family systems therapy.

"Perception is awareness shaped by belief. Beliefs "control" perceptions rewrite perception, and you rewrite the field of the genes and its behavioral outcome." Bruce Lipton

2) RE-Feeding the Brain and the Body: Integrate and Implement

The connection between the body and the brain is bi-directional and involves communication via cell signaling throughout the nervous system. Through this bidirectional relationship, signals from the brain can influence the gut, and visceral messages can affect brain function. The autonomic nervous system is a component of the peripheral nervous system that contains three anatomically distinct divisions: sympathetic, parasympathetic, and enteric.

The importance of the enteric nervous system is highlighted here. Dr. Andrew D.Huberman, Ph.D., neuroscientist and tenured professor in the Department of Neurobiology at the Stanford University School of Medicine, director of the Huberman Lab, states that "We sense ourselves and our inner biochemistry landscape through the process of enteroception via the enteric nervous system, which mirrors to us the internal state of the body."

The most available way that the brain gets in touch with the nerve cells is through neurotransmitters. Neurotransmitters are chemicals that transmit nerve energy and are chemical messengers derived from amino acids in the diet; therefore, the concentration of amino acids in the diet will change the levels of neurotransmitters in the body. Neurotransmitters are primarily found in the brain, heart, and gastrointestinal system. Neurotransmitter production also relies on supporting nutrients for their output. Therefore, any nutritional deficiencies relevant to neurotransmitter production will also negatively affect by limiting these necessary neurotransmitters' output and availability. Specific nutrients include an array of five to nineteen amino acids and glucose needed for feeding the brain and the nervous system, states Julia Ross, MA, the author of the Diet Cure, The Craving Cure, and The Mood Cure and a pioneer in using nutritional therapy to treat eating disorders, addictions, and mood problems.

The enteric nervous system further detects the availability or lack of these nutrients, which could either hinder the expression of a healthy mood, sleep, focus, and energy or propel it beyond survival, an encouraging place to be. We cannot have the attention of the brain when not fed correctly. The imperativeness of providing for the brain first and the crucial role that the dietary proteins and amino acid supplementation play in that capacity and the prevention of relapse is the cornerstone of Christina Vaselec's teachings and coaching; a licensed psychotherapist, the founder and director of the Academy for Addiction and Mental Health Nutrition

---

"Feed the Brain First" Christina Vaselec

Christina notes that we could be just a "personalized amino acid therapy" plan away from feeding our brains and supporting the prevention of relapse from addiction.

The nervous system contains over forty neurotransmitters, with more than a hundred neurotransmitters identified to date. The principal neurotransmitters related to brain function include Serotonin, GABA, Dopamine and, Norepinephrine. While Dopamine and Norepinephrine belong to the excitatory class of neurotransmitters, Serotonin and GABA are categorized as inhibitory neurotransmitters. You can think of these distinct differences as the Yin and Yang of the brain. Dopamine and norepinephrine have excitatory effects on the neuron, increasing the likelihood that the neuron will fire an action potential, hence the Yin. Serotonin and GABA have inhibitory effects on the neuron, decreasing the probability of firing an action, hence the Yang. Neurotransmitters require supporting nutrients such as vitamin C, B6, B3, zinc, magnesium, and additional micro-nutrients to be produced by the body, and additionally, the whole system will be negatively affected under any dysmetabolic conditions. Endorphin depletion addiction Tyrosine and L-phenylalanine are two primary amino acids used to help support dopamine production. Omega-3 fatty acids include ALA, EPA, and DHA, sourced from marine fish and algae, are highly supportive of neurotransmitter activity, specifically dopamine. Omega-3's support the brain's neuroplasticity which refers to the brain's malleability to change and adapt to an experience. Furthermore, any alterations in the number of neurotransmitter receptors, damages caused by toxins located on a synapse (the junction between nerve cells), will also negatively affect the passing of an electrical or chemical signal in the brain, therefore hindering a state of "whole-brain activity" and thinking.

3) From Pleasure to Pain, the Risks and Rewards

Dopamine is perhaps the most significant neurotransmitter related to our daily experiences since it stimulates motivation, desire, cravings, satisfaction, and a sense of well-being.

"Dopamine lies at the heart of addiction in all things and is optimal for pretty much everything except for sleep." Andrew Huberman

Dopamine rises above baseline with the consumption of refined carbohydrates, caffeine, sugar, and chocolate. Nicotine, coffee, and alcohol also raise dopamine; however, the effects are short-lived. Amphetamine increases Dopamine baseline by tenfold, Opioids increase dopamine baseline by two and half times. Enjoyable exercise also increases Dopamine levels by two and half times, reported being more in some cases due to its subjective nature and long-lasting effects. Social engagements that promote bonding, excitable quality conversations, daily journaling, and gratitude are also considered dopamine-evoking activities.

Individuals who can keep a high dopamine baseline do not require high doses of dopamine release to feel well. Dopamine reward prediction error states that one is likely to experience a dopamine plummeting level when certain repetitive activities become a routine and thus lose their intensity to produce the same amount of dopamine as before. Usage of social media in excess is one example of dopamine reward prediction error. Intermittent dopamine release via a periodic reward schedule has proven to be a lifestyle activity that helps maintain a high dopamine baseline. Leveraging dopamine through behaviors such as cold showers and immersing oneself in cold water helps increase dopamine baselines while increasing norepinephrine and cortisol above baseline. Another practice for increasing dopamine baselines would be to limit enjoyable exercises without adding any other dopamine-evoking methods at the same time. Adrenaline, also called epinephrine-cortisol, is manufactured from dopamine in the body, and norepinephrine is converted into adrenaline in the brain. Adrenaline converts into cortisol during high-intensity activities that may not be pleasurable and counterproductive in individuals with challenges producing adequate cortisol and is often referred to as a condition called "adrenal fatigue." This condition highlights the importance of a personalized physical activity regimen during such conditions.

Genetic Influences:

The genetic, epigenetic, and neurobiological bases of addiction have advanced the science of addiction and will continue to do so as genes influence the number and type of receptors in the brain, how quickly the body metabolizes drugs and how well the body responds to different medications.

Reward Deficiency Syndrome (RDS) was discovered by Dr. Kenneth Blum in 1996. The term refers to an inborn chemical imbalance that alters the intercellular signaling in the brain's reward process and can manifest itself as one or more behavioral disorders. It Is characterized by a genetically influenced deficiency in D2 receptor sites and affects the entire reward pathway. This trait leads to multiple drug-seeking behaviors. This is so because **alcohol, cocaine, heroin, marijuana, nicotine, and glucose** all-cause activation and neuronal release of brain damage, which could heal the abnormal cravings. Low dopamine activity results in a lack of everyday enjoyment. This genetically identified condition leads to a full range of addictive behavior throughout an addicted family system. Understanding an individual's specific vulnerabilities through genetic testing provides the ability to both prevent and enhance recovery by actively modifying an individual's environment, including the use of dietary supplements tailored to an individual's vulnerabilities.

4) Repeat, Regenerate, Restore: Intermittent fasting and the benefits to brain health

Step four includes re-visiting steps one and two after a given period to re-evaluate other factors involving those steps that need additional intervention. Any initial variation suggested in those steps must be continued for a period before it can be re-evaluated. Most individuals may have multiple conditions that need attention and intervention.

Two main metabolic factors highlighted address metabolic fitness and the body's ability to be an efficient calorie-burning and energy-producing machinery. Extreme fluctuations in blood sugar harm mood, energy, and mental sharpness. In addition, supporting healthy blood sugar levels protects the nervous system from long-term damages that may not be reversible. It is not unusual that food options and dietary plans change throughout an individual's healing, regenerating process. Since everyone has a unique bio-identical individuality, considering possible allergies, intolerances, micro and macro distribution, cultural and personal preferences, creating a one-size-fits-all feeding plan is almost impossible. However, the principle of restoring and managing blood sugar remains constant across the board. The regeneration of overall cellular health achieved through a personalized meal plan, gut repair, and the elimination of various toxicants stand as principles to hold for most individuals living in our industrialized world. Ketogenic diets switch the metabolic state of an individual from a sugar-burning state to a fat-burning state. It renews and rebuilds the body from the cellular level.

" Better living through chemistry still requires better living."
Andrew Huberman

The human body is highly resilient and can restore and regenerate itself in a proper health conducive environment. It takes many years of biochemical, nutritional deficiency for an organ or a biological system to become hypo-functional and ultimately fail. Prevention, therefore, should be the centralized focus for sustaining a healthy body and halting the process of aging.

The integration of all of which was shared is what defines a functionally integrated style of living. A kind that becomes a part of oneself, like the heart and the brain.

I hope this chapter will serve as a source of hope and empowerment to help transcend what is and integrate what could be.

"Your health is personal, and It is the only thing that should be taken personal." Ayleen Hacopian

So remember, As above so below!

ABOUT THE AUTHOR
AYLEEN HACOPIAN

Ayleen Hacopian, MS, RD, CAN, CRNC, is a Medical Nutrition Specialist and a Lifestyle Therapy Guide

Ayleen holds a Master of Science Degree in Nutritional Science and a postgraduate Certification in Alternative Nutrition from the Department of Kinesiology from California State University, Los Angeles, where she has resided since 1979. She has accomplished her Dietetic Internship at Public Health Foundation Enterprises, White Memorial Hospital, and Children's Hospital in Los Angeles. She is further certified as a Recovery Nutrition Coach from the Academy of Addiction and Mental Health Nutrition.

Her past professional experiences of 33 years include:
• Public health nutrition promotion.
• Medical nutrition therapy.
• Disease prevention education.
• Detoxification and regeneration.
• Therapeutic lifestyle counseling.
• Therapeutic and functional food plans.

Her expertise lies in understanding the hierarchy of the body's needs in the refeeding, regenerating, rejuvenating, detoxifying, and healing. The functional and therapeutic approaches to nutrition and lifestyle assume that foods deliver biochemical and energetic information that engages at the molecular level throughout the body's constituents to support the metabolism—immune function, mental, emotional, and physical fitness. Lifestyle, quality food intake, daily and consistent habits have proven to be the foundation for delaying dis-ease and disease throughout an individual's lifespan.

With the emergence and advancements in epigenetics, nutrigenomics, functional laboratory testing, and pharmaco-genetic testing, Ayleen contributes to the personalized-functional-integrated healthcare model by working together with various clinicians and health practitioners in a complementary fashion to bring about her vitality-creating programs that also address nutritional deficiencies brought about by disease conditions and medications. Ayleen speaks of principles of healthy meal plans independent of their "type" or culture, constructs personalized meals, nutritional and herbal supplement plans including what she calls "Functional Super Meals" to provide a nourishing environment inside and out - within and without.

Ayleen is looking forward to a new and improved future of an ever-evolving world by further contributing towards the betterment and growth of healthier humankind in the present and for future generations.

www.Quantumlynourished.com

2

CELIA LOUISE
ACKNOWLEDGING YOUR INSTINCTS

*D*o you have an ache inside of you that won't leave you alone? Perhaps you have a successful career, family, friends and look like you have it all together. Yet, deep inside, you are crying. You can't quite understand why. You did all of the things. You have your education, career, a relationship, family, and friends. Most of the time, you are happy, but there is an ache that releases itself as loneliness, tears, anger, or sadness that you cannot explain. You think your life is in need of a reset, but you are not sure how to reset it.

Your natural instincts are telling you something. But what is the message?

You fill it with shopping, tv, holidays, surfing the internet, eating or drinking. Perhaps you change jobs, move, buy a new car, or leave a relationship. It may happen when a partner leaves you.

You think you have solved your "problem" because the ache is quiet for a while, but soon you realize it is there still. This ache releases itself at the worst times. Sometimes the tears flow in public, and you run to the bathroom to hide. Sometimes the anger is directed toward someone you love, and you wonder why your easy, happy personality disappeared? Some days, you lay crying at home, unable to get yourself together for work or a family dinner.

This ache plays in the background of your life until one day you realize you need to do something about it. The ache in your heart is a response to not acknowledging your instincts. Suppressing your instincts blocks your energy and leads to a lack of joy and lack of clarity.

This is what happened to me. To the surprise of almost everyone we knew, my ex-husband and I mutually ended our marriage. I felt that if I stayed on our farm one more day, I would surely die from a deep unhappiness that I could not understand, and neither could he. I said goodbye to the man I had married at 21. I gave my university aged daughter a very teary hug. I went out to our farmyard and kissed my dogs and horses goodbye. I drove to the city, and I got on a plane and flew to Pakistan.

I dedicated myself even more to my work. Helping others has long been my motto. This is my thing. I love the adrenaline of being called to action to help others. I had worked in conflict zones for over 10 years, and it felt really good to think I was helping others. At the time, I believed I was doing my best to build a more peaceful world. In all honesty, Pakistan was my version of the famous book Eat, Pray, Love by Elizabeth Gilbert. She was smart. She went to save herself, while I was still ignoring myself and poured my energy into saving others. One day I received a call to inform me that eight of our local medical staff were kidnapped by the Taliban along the Afghanistan border. It was three long months of negotiations and sleepless nights until they were safely returned. My adrenaline was going full speed.

The adrenaline rush of helping others kept the ache away and distracted me from replenishing and nurturing myself for the entire year. When I returned to Canada, so did the ache. One year later, I woke up one day thinking about ending my life—I envisioned jumping off my 18th floor balcony. This is out of character for me, and

I didn't really think I would do this, but that thought was my call to action.

I called my doctor and a therapist friend. I didn't like their suggestions to take anti-depression drugs and go to a therapist, although given their professions, it made sense! I stayed in bed for three months, unable to go to work or to see friends. I went from sad to mad. I recall being so pissed off that my body did not come with an owner's manual as my car did. I wanted to know how to operate it for peak performance, not for sports but for life, to find the root cause of why I felt like this, not simply fix the symptoms. When I got mad enough, I finally dragged myself out of bed and started looking for the kind of help I felt would work best for me.

I hired my first life coach, and the questions she asked made me think deeply about the meaning of life and rediscovering joy. Soul assignments opened my perceptions. Although I had always believed in helping others, "receiving help" was a new lesson for me. Life coaching emerged from the world of professionals wanting to better their performance and skills in their field, such as sports, acting, business, and motivating others. I wanted to get better at what I desired, what I yearned for, to love my life, to regain confidence, live authentically, and follow my instincts. I observed that I am very skilled at motivating others to live their truth while unknowingly hiding my own truth.

I continued my medical leave from work and hopped on another plane. I studied Yoga, Reiki, and Meditation in Mexico. Soon after, I quit my job and studied Tantra in California. During this time, I felt I was becoming "smarter," but the truth is these practices initiated a reset and reconnection to the source of our energy and consciousness, which holds the creative wisdom of all things.

At the time, I was both attracted and repelled by the words, "all answers are inside of you" and "we are all energy." I let go of my judgement and let curiosity take over as I had something new to be curious about—me! I discovered the essential connection of body, mind, and heart and how they became disconnected as I denied my own needs and distracted myself by externalizing "caring." I began to explore who I was with a curiosity I hadn't accessed since childhood. I discovered self-love. The desire for things became less, and the desire for experiences increased. I lost my fear of not having or being "enough."

My favourite lessons were about resetting my energy, perceiving my instincts, and accessing universal wisdom through the practice of meditation. I began to understand my energy, what it was and what it wasn't. That energy cannot be destroyed, it can only be transformed. And transform I did. I learned to say no when previously, I would say yes. I felt and understood my natural instincts for the first time since I was a child. Blocked energy channels are the barrier to feeling and acknowledging your instincts.

Here are three main energy blocks:

1) **How you breathe:** I wish I were kidding! I didn't realize how often I held my breath until I studied tantra. This breath pattern was a result of being told to be quiet while being raped at the age of 12 by my seemingly kind and handsome camp counsellor. I held my breath that night and never realized the chain reaction. The Catholic belief system I was raised in contributed to my feelings of deep shame from this and I never spoke about it to anyone for decades. I continued to hold my breath when stress hit me, and my normal breathing pattern was shallow breaths, my locked-in trauma response from that night.

There are many breath courses available now, but my favourites are the ancient practices from the wisdom traditions in yoga and tantra. This changed my life, my energy, and my access to divine wisdom, and I love to teach these techniques. The most important practice to master is deep, slow breathing. This is essential because it tones the vagus nerve, which has over a million nerve endings in the gut. A slow breath pattern soothes the nervous system, allowing the body to assist in mastering emotional intelligence. We need to do more than tone our muscles, our nerves need toning too! Think about the stress you feel in your gut when something upsetting occurs in your life or those "gut" feelings you get that inform you if you are safe or unsafe.

Research shows that the vagus nerve loses its resilience when we become stuck in the emotions of our experiences. The problem is not the actual events but how we hold the emotional residue in our bodies, and in particular, in the vagus nerve. Habitual, shallow breathing weakens the vagus nerve. A healthy vagus nerve will speed up the heart when you sense danger, then shake it off when no danger is present. Chest breathing stimulates anxiety and emotional imbalance, while belly breathing stimulates relaxation. Your vagus nerve is key to your resilience. Trusting your gut means trusting your vagus nerve. Gut instinct is transferred to your brain via the vagus nerve.

Ask yourself, how do you breathe? Practice getting to six breaths per minute by breathing in to a count of five and out to a count of five. Proper breathing supplies more oxygen to our bloodstream and makes more oxygen available to our brains. More oxygen is proven to improve brain function, physical energy, mental clarity, and productivity. It is essential to feeling your instincts.

2) How many trapped emotions you hold: Trapped emotions manifested physically for me as a hard ball in my solar plexus that grew in size from a baseball to a bowling ball over twenty years. Nothing showed up on x-rays, but it felt painful and real. Energy healing removed this painful ball, this physical response. Removing my manifested negative emotions from unprocessed life events changed my life.

The thing about emotions is that they can be located both in your conscious mind and your subconscious mind. If you are able to process the emotions you feel easily, this pattern of thinking remains in your conscious mind, and this fosters resilience. If there are unprocessed emotions keeping you stuck, they may be there from a time when you were unable to process them. Like I was, at the age of 12. Unprocessed emotions are likely hiding out in your subconscious mind, inherited, prenatal, or absorbed, and this is where energetic removal is needed. What is not helpful is ignoring them because they remain as unprocessed emotional energy that accumulates in your body and may erupt into anger, overwhelm, stress or disease. This is how instincts are blocked.

Ask yourself, how well you process your emotions? Recognize that your words become your thoughts, and your thoughts inform your emotions. Emotions are the energy behind learning, decision-making, creativity, relationships, wealth, and health. Recognizing your emotions can help you release them rather than bury or ignore them.

3) The limiting beliefs of others that condition the way you act and speak: I did not even know I was filled with limiting beliefs because I thought that walking away from the church and choosing a different path than my parents was all I needed to do. So wrong. I had to uncover, remove and replace the beliefs I held about relationships, sex and money. This changed my perceptions and led me to insights that I had missed before. Examine your limiting beliefs. Do you have limiting beliefs from your childhood that make you feel like you aren't capable or that make you feel guilt, shame, or other negative emotions? Or perhaps you have limiting beliefs based on your culture, religion, or education that make you feel unable to participate in life as you would like to because of certain learned behaviours, expectations, or perceptions. Limiting beliefs also are created from your past experiences. These may make you feel like you can't do something because it's simply too hard for you. None of these are true. The only limits you have are those you create with your thoughts. Imagine the life you desire. If you didn't have any limiting beliefs, what would your life look like?

Ask yourself, do you trust your gut feelings, your natural instincts? If your energy system is clogged with the beliefs of others, it is hard to access the authentic intelligence based in your energy system and create energetic alignment in yourself.

Opening my energy channels led me to feeling my instincts again. I discovered we didn't need magic, we are magical. We are all created with stardust in us. Every atom of oxygen in our lungs, carbon in our muscles, calcium in our bones, and iron in our blood was created inside a star before our earth was born.

You don't need to be fixed—you need to reconnect to the source energy and wisdom of the universe. When you understand how strong the connection is, you will start feeling your instincts, connecting to your soul, and allowing it to co-create your life with you. Your instincts lead the way to your soul, and your soul leads you home to your heart. Your heart is 5000 x magnetically stronger than your brain, and it sends more messages to your brain than your brain sends to your heart. This is the seat of your natural instincts.

Consciously take five minutes every day to simply place your hands on your heart and breathe deeply and slowly. Placing your hands on your heart helps to release oxytocin, the feel-good hormone. Breathe deeply. Breathe Slowly. Connect to your instincts to allow their messages to reach you. When you can clearly hear or feel your instincts, you will be able to confidently choose love and kindness over fear, curiosity over judgment, and abundance over lack.

Understanding my instincts lead me to universal wisdom. I explored spirituality and the divine because I felt them but didn't know how to talk about them. The church of my childhood no longer resonated with me. Now I see that a spiritual path is simply the path of love rather than fear. People tend to live their lives from one of those two paths, fear or love. Love is an energy that is so much more than romantic love. Love is felt in the deep connection to the energy and consciousness of our universe. This wisdom gifted me with the ability to know that nothing is personal and to understand that everyone is on their own path of discovery. The more I lead from a place of love, the more I observe the same in others around me.

Seeking this path of love led me to meditation. Meditation leads to love, yet not all meditation is meant for people living full lives with families and careers. Too many people have been taught to meditate in the renunciation path of monks and nuns. This is a great path if you want to live like a monk or a nun. I definitely did not and found that this meditation style bored me (sit very still, empty your mind). I wanted to embrace all my senses, not dull them!

I discovered that there is a householder path from the tantra tradition of meditation. This enlivens the senses, is joyful and eye-opening. It is described as both the joy and terror of meeting your soul, and it has quickly become an essential activity in my clients' lives.

Meditation is how I access the universal wisdom that people from all walks of life access to develop their musical, athletic, business genius, and Nobel Peace Prize discoveries. Wisdom is different than intelligence. Intelligence is gained through practice and the study of what is known. Wisdom is the energetic connection people use to download discoveries or channel new insights and perspectives previously unknown to them. Wisdom is knowledge before thought interferes.

The point of meditation is to open yourself to the possibilities of your life. To be able to clear your energy on a daily basis, even if only for five minutes. Many successful business leaders or scientists have shared that when they want to know the answer to a problem they are working on, they meditate until the answer becomes clear to them. The key to meditation is knowing that there are at least 112 gateways into accessing the consciousness of the universe. They are instinctive, and you may already be practicing some of these without realizing it. Some meditators may do something different every day or change their method if it becomes stale to them. Movement, being in nature, or lying down are all gateways to bring you to a meditative state. Some days I will get an answer to a question or a new insight during my meditation. On other days, no new insights come, but I have a lovely feeling of merging with universal energy.

The deep dive into myself led me to become a Life Coach, which means I guide and assist people in finding their energy leaks, release energetic blocks, reset their energy, engage with their instincts and come home to their hearts. Most of the people I work with have a "happy on the outside" look to them, as I did. They have a great life that seemed to work until they acknowledged that it didn't. For some reason, they feel sad, empty, or angry inside and have made the decision to "fix" this. When a person invites me into their reality, we begin to reset their energy. They move toward reconnecting to their heart, the source energy, and wisdom of our universe. Here, they rediscover their instincts.

This process leads to an expanded energetic vibration increasingly moving us into the flow of life rather than struggling against it. This is our most authentic way of being. Something like being in love without needing another person around, you discover you love your life again, and this time you understand why and how to return there anytime you get lost.

Instincts are your innate power and will guide you into energetic alignment & flow. To make decisions with your instincts, learn to feel for a full body yes or no. For me, a full body yes is a burst of energy & excitement in my solar plexus and heart chakras. A full body no is a tense or even sick to my stomach feeling in my solar plexus chakra and tension in my throat chakra.

The way you feel inside is your personal navigation system. When your body is talking to you, listen. Acknowledging your instincts reduces the overthinking and second guessing that leads to self-doubt, lack of clarity and seriously reduces your joy.

Do you feel that your instincts have been shut down?

ABOUT THE AUTHOR
CELIA LOUISE

Celia Louise is the Creator of Champagne Chakra Coaching. She helps her clients understand & connect to their powerful energy field, helping them clear their path back to their innate energy & wisdom. Celia has a Masters' Degree in Human Security and Peacebuilding, and Certifications in HeartMath, Brain Story, The Emotion Code, Tantra, Yoga, Reiki, Instinctive Meditation & Conscious Reading. Celia loves to share the practices that radically reset her energy, joy, and confidence after a mid-career crisis. The unanswered ache in Celia's heart brought her to seek out energy healing and life coaching for herself.

That we live in a connected energy field has fascinated Celia since her days of teaching others to farm organically, in Canada, California, & Indonesia. Her second career focused on international peace, human rights and humanitarian aid in the conflict & post conflict zones of El Salvador, Indonesia, Pakistan and Rwanda, teaching her the truth of human resilience. She shares her best practices so you can live and love your best life.

www.celialouise.com/

3

CRYSTAL RASMUSSEN
LIVING YOUR LEGACY

HEALING ANCESTRAL TRAUMA FREES YOURSELF, YOUR
FAMILY, AND FUTURE GENERATIONS

Standing against the trunk of my favorite crab apple tree filled with fresh new leaves, I cried uncontrollably, screaming at the Universe, begging for something to change. Everything about my life felt hard. I was miserable, unhappy, and filled with self-doubt. I felt disconnected from my body, the Earth, my purpose, and life itself. As a single mom, struggle, survival, confusion, and fear controlled my life at every turn.

"If this is the way life is going to be, then I don't want to be here anymore!" I screamed at the Universe from a state of desperation and hopelessness.

I couldn't imagine continuing living the way I had been. A string of broken and failed relationships scattered behind me—all being extremely co-dependent and adding to my story that I am unlovable and unworthy. Since I was a young girl, I believed that something was wrong with me, that I was broken. After all, I never fit in, and it felt as if I couldn't do anything right. The fear of judgement from others made my self-judgement even more harsh.

Depression hit hard. I could barely pull myself out of bed each morning.

The journey of unhealthy relationships and my desire to seek the truth had led me to explore energy healing. Yet nothing I learned, studied, or did, seemed to have a lasting result to eliminate the thoughts and feelings I experienced so deeply.

I yearned to feel alive. I longed to smile. I wanted to enjoy living. I wanted and needed to engage with the seen and the unseen realms. I was seeking to discover my purpose. I knew there was more to life than what I had been experiencing. I knew life was about enjoying living as a Spirit in a body on this beautiful playground we call Earth.

But I wasn't doing that.

Once all the tears I could shed soaked into the soil at my feet near that crab apple tree, I did what I always did. I pulled my bootstraps up and went about my day.

Little did I know at the time that the heaviness I felt, the thoughts, the feelings, and the pain and suffering I carried deep within my cells, were not only conditioning and limiting beliefs from childhood and my own wounding, but they were also ancestral trauma that had been passed down from one generation to the next.

The Great Spirit, my Ancestors, guides, and helpers on the other side, heard my plea that day. They weren't going to allow me to leave my young children. They weren't going to let me avoid my lessons or not fulfil the mission I came to do here on Earth.

They showed up in full force to guide me on the way, adding a spark of life and desire to my heart by randomly sharing a website on my computer, leading me to say "Yes" to a program that changed my life.

As a seeker, I've always searched for truth. I longed to get to the root of issues and unravel the pain points to bring you back to who you truly are—at the Soul level. When I discovered Soul Therapy School®, my entire body resonated with what was awakening within me. My cells vibrated, and tears streamed down my cheeks as if I was coming home to myself. It spoke to me on a level beyond anything I'd experienced before.

The problem? My fear got in the way. The investment was large—beyond what I could comprehend at the time. As a single mother, I could barely pay my bills. And at the time, I thought that investing in myself was selfish, irresponsible, and darn right stupid. After all, how could I justify spending that money on something when I didn't even know what would come out of it.

I felt hopeless. Knowing that this investment was going to lead me to the growth and evolution my Soul craved, yet, feeling like it was impossible to attain it.

I nearly gave up.

Thinking I was destined to live a life of struggle, confusion, disconnected from my purpose, and simply put, in extreme unhappiness, I was devastated. Everything I was searching for felt out of my reach. Within that feeling of limitation, constriction, and unworthiness, I made a declaration.

Something had to change. I decided that I was done being a victim to outside circumstances, my excuses, and the pain points that felt very real in my life.

Life was about living. Not about surviving.

I promised myself in that moment that no matter what, I was more important than the beliefs, lies, fear, the money, and all the excuses I told myself.

From the very core of my being, I claimed a spot in that school as mine.

Activating every cell in my being, I decided to do whatever it took to enroll.

I committed. Fully.

I listened to the guidance. I took action. I stretched into places that felt uncomfortable.

It was scary. It was nerve-racking. I questioned and doubted myself and my decision nearly every step of the way. But I continued putting one foot in front of the other, moving towards my goal, and stayed committed to myself and the vision of living and loving life.

Within my YES, doors opened. The money came. New connections were made.

Truth awakened within me.

As I studied with my mentor, the founder of Generational Healing® and Soul Therapy School®, Deborah Skye King, life began changing. Hope filled my heart again.

During one teaching, in particular, she asked me, "What is your legacy?"

As I sat there pondering this question, I knew my legacy wasn't a million dollars or some fancy invention. It wasn't *stuff*. It was something close and personal to my heart.

Suddenly it came to me.

What do I want my children to know before I die? What do I want to teach them?

"To fully live one's truth, no matter what," I proudly stated.

"I want to teach my children to engage with life. To embrace every moment. To make choices that support their Soul in feeling alive and connected. To express their truth. To show up as themselves, regardless of what others might think. To be conscious and mindful of their needs. To live full out in whatever way that looks like for them to love life and be happy."

Not only do I want to leave this for my children and future generations, I want this to be a message to others in the world. It feels important. Just the idea inspired me in a multitude of ways.

I began dreaming, "*What would the world look like if humanity started living and expressing themselves from this place? What if the 'shoulds', obligations, limitations, and fears were eliminated, and people could fully be themselves? What if people were in the present moment, engaged, with their heart open, and felt alive doing what inspired their Soul? What if they stopped fearing the judgements and making excuses?*"

BAMMMM! It hit me like a ton of bricks.

I slowly stuttered, in realization at that moment, "I'm not living my truth at all. "Tears filled my eyes, my body shifted, and my mind floated back to the moment I was crying in desperation under the crab apple tree where all I wanted to do was live better, be happier, express more, and operate from a space of feeling alive and connected to my purpose and truth.

Up until that point, I had spent my days in survival mode, focusing on what others needed from me, the box I was supposed to fit in, how the bills would get paid that month, how I could support my kids in the best way possible, chasing love and feeling unsafe in my body and the world. I pushed people, opportunities, love, and life away from me. My heart had been closed out of fear of being hurt and rejected. I had been rejecting life. I had been rejecting myself, my truth.

I was living the only way I knew how. Deep in fear, with my world small and constricted, terrified to expand and try something new. At most, I was operating at 2% of my authentic expression and fully living my truth.

Thoughts like *"stay small","* *don't rock the boat", "keep quiet", "you don't know what you're talking about", "you're too sensitive", "I can't",* filled my mind and repeated on a loop.

My upbringing, religion, culture, society, and generational beliefs and traumas dictated my thoughts, my feelings, my choices, and my physical reality. I was stuck in victim mode, deep in survival, where fear, doubt, and limitation controlled me.

This epiphany supported me in making a decision to no longer allow the patterns of the past to continue to control me. I strongly claimed from within the core of my being I was going to allow truth and freedom to emanate from me with every choice I made. It wasn't easy. It stretched my comfort zone. I doubted. I questioned. I probably even looked crazy to the outside world. But it didn't matter. I needed to honor and respect my Soul in a way I never had before. And I started to feel happier in this new alignment.

I started saying yes to myself more, which led me into the next training with my mentor, where I finally discovered my purpose and fell in love with life and myself in a whole new way.

The 13 Mystical Wisdom Teachings and Generational Healing® with Deborah Skye is where I learned the pain and suffering, I carried, the patterns I lived out and felt I couldn't change, and the engrained fear and self-doubt wasn't only mine. It had been passed down through the family lineage from one generation to the next. I chose it before I was born, and I was here to heal it for myself, my family, my children, my future grandchildren, my Ancestors, and the Earth.

My mind was blown. My heart opened. And I started engaging with direction and purpose with the seen and the unseen.

I started living with love, freedom, and joy. I felt alive again, connected, on purpose, and more embodied and present than I ever had been before.

I began to see a larger picture. I realized we borrow the Earth from our future generations and started questioning how do we want to leave it for them? I pondered how healing ancestral trauma would create a ripple effect in the world, making a difference for us now and for our descendants.

I saw the importance of healing our Ancestors. How grateful they are to receive that healing and offer it to those that are carrying the trauma in this timeline. I saw the difference healing our Ancestors makes for our children of today, future children, and grandchildren many generations forward.

I dedicated myself to be an example for my children and grandchildren. Remembering, with every choice I make, they watch me, they see me, and they either learn conditioning, inherit trauma, or they are inspired to make a difference in the world and be in love with their life, honoring the sacred in every moment.

Now I focus on living my purpose and supporting families in healing the pain and suffering that continues to be passed down from one generation to another. We are here to make a difference for our future. We are here to free our grandchildren from the traumas our ancient bloodline experienced. We are here to stand in integrity, love, truth, and freedom. It is our honor to have this role for us, generations past and generations to come.

The experience I had at the Generational Healing® Certification Training altered me. It showed me my purpose, to LIVE my life and stay connected to myself and my truth. I came home to myself. How I show up daily changed. Who I was being was transformed.

I found me. My confidence, my worth, my voice grew. Life changed. *This is what I want to share with my children and future generations,* I thought.

I no longer wanted them to carry the hurt and trauma I put them through as I raised them. I no longer wanted my grandchildren to experience their parents the same way my children experienced me, or how I experienced my parents. I wanted to free them and my future generations from having to experience the pain and suffering that had been passed down within my family lineage that affected each of us mentally, emotionally, physically and spiritually.

I began traveling, exploring, connecting, and experiencing this new freedom. I created an intimate relationship with self, the sacred world around me, and the unseen realm. I discovered my purpose.

From that moment, it's been a continual expansion into more of my truth, more of my freedom, more of my destiny. That choice is something I'm very proud of and hold deeply within my heart to remind myself of the power of commitment to Self.

I learned that no matter what the "outside" world might say, the thoughts that hold you back and the fears that show up only stop you if you let them.

I learned that I didn't have to be a victim to anything, including all the things that I've been told. I didn't have to allow money, excuses, fears, or anything else to control me.

In that recognition, I took back my Power.

When your heart speaks, you have the opportunity to toss aside all of the outside noise, the excuses, and the fears and say Yes to you. Within that, you empower yourself and step on a path aligned to your Soul's calling.

Sadly, most of us aren't fully living our lives based on what our Soul craves. Instead, our choices are based on fear. We don't take that chance. We don't pick up the phone because we are afraid of rejection. We pass on forgiving in fear of being hurt again. We don't start that business because we are afraid of failing or being laughed at. We don't quit the job we hate because we believe there is no other option. We don't take that trip because we can't lose the job we hate. We don't become the healer we long to be out of fear of not being or knowing enough. The list goes on and on.

We put off living until tomorrow. What if there wasn't another tomorrow?

What if you were no longer going to be here on Earth in 1 year? 5 years? 10 years? Would your choices in life be different? Would your daily activities change?

Life is made up of moments, and each of these creates our legacy. These moments are the marks left behind by us on earth, the memory we leave for our loved ones when our time is up.

These ideas left me with a few questions: How are we living our lives right now? Are we embracing it, or are we pushing it away and telling ourselves we'll do it later?

Are we willing to take a risk and begin to fully live our lives, embracing the short time we have here on this amazing planet?

Are we willing to connect deeply with our Ancestors, heal the traumas that have been passed down to create a better tomorrow, and heal across timelines?

Are we willing to answer our Soul's calling?

Are you repeating patterns from your family and generations past?

I invite you to discover who you are by living fully with love and intention in each moment.

Here are a few simple questions to help us discover what we could do differently and begin to live fully:

1.   What in our life are you struggling with? What seems to not be working? In order to fully live, we have to be able to identify all the places where we are not honoring and celebrating who we authentically are. That means being really honest with ourselves on what isn't working for us, no matter what that might be.

2.   What does your Soul crave? What do you yearn to experience? This is the fun part. You get to imagine anything. The sky is the limit.

Do you dream of hopping on a plane and spending a week in another country? Do you long to do mission work in the world? Have you desired to go back to school and get a degree? Launching a new invention or brand? What about curling up for an entire day with your lover?

3.   What is stopping you? What excuses do you tell yourself? What resources do you feel are not available, and what can you do to change that? This brings in awareness and helps you get really clear on where you aren't embracing your life fully.

I invite you to break the cycles of inherent generational trauma. Choose for you. Honor your Soul. You are worth it!

ABOUT THE AUTHOR
CRYSTAL RASMUSSEN

Crystal Rasmussen, a professionally trained and certified Generational Healing® Teacher and Spiritual Guide supports you in releasing pain and suffering from your ancient bloodline stored within your genetic lineage to heal you today through in person and distance sessions. When she first connected to an ancestor while facilitating a session during her apprenticeship training, she found it to be one of the most humbling, rewarding experiences, she'd ever had. She became more present, confident, and grounded within herself while finally experiencing her spiritual gifts in a new and exciting way, altering the way she perceived the world.

Her profound experience had such an impact that she knew she had finally discovered her purpose, leading her to change the trajectory of her life. With her passion for healing inherent family trauma and working with the Ancestors she dedicated herself to sharing this powerful ancestral healing with others. Her Apprentice Training for Generational Healing® began with the 13 Mystical Wisdom Teachings. She has been teaching the 7-day Generational Healing® Certification Training in the US and Canada for the past six years. Crystal guides women who want to serve humanity, awaken their spiritual gifts and release pain and trauma that is passed down from one generation to another to heal the world.

You can learn more about the training, book a session or connect with her at her Website:
www.crystalrasmussen.com

4

DEBBIE SQUIZZERO
FROM SURVIVING TO THRIVING

We are all unique. We all have a story. We all have emotional baggage. There is no denying it. Our journey here in the physical world is unique to us and only us. It is filled with pop quizzes we never saw coming and tests we didn't even know we had to study for, and yet, here we are showing up each and every day for our story in this classroom we refer to as life or the Universe. Our learning here in the physical world is for our soul's growth and evolution. Our unique soul experience, lessons, and story are written by you and for you. Do not compare your soul's journey or experiences to anyone else. Your lessons, learnings, and teachings are a unique set of circumstances, experiences, and situations belonging to you and only you.

Begin to think of your story and your journey here in the physical world as compared to a snowflake or a fingerprint. No two are alike. No two souls will experience the same exact journey. My unique story centers on the concepts of worthiness and learning to love myself, embracing the true essence of who I am after denying it for many years and finally embracing it after a stress-induced mental and emotional breakdown. I am a professional Psychic Medium, but it would be close to 20 years before I fully embrace that title and concept of who I am, know I am worthy of it, and own it loud and proud. This is my story.

My life is absolutely nothing the way I thought it would be or as I envisioned it to be. I pictured myself being a wife, a mother, having a couple of kids, and a family dog. I would be living with my wonderful and supportive husband in a home we purchased. I saw myself being a teacher until the age of retirement. I have been an early childhood special education teacher for 22 years, teaching Kindergarten and First grade students. Looking back now, my soul had other plans for this lifetime or incarnation. Being a teacher was my "place card" so to speak. It held my space or life purpose like a place card at an event holds your table space until I was really ready to own and embrace my Mediumship skills, talents, and abilities on a full-time professional level.

None of what I envisioned about my traditional life came to fruition, and that is ok. I have learned on this Earth School journey, which is not an easy one at all, that when we surrender to a higher power, it will never steer you wrong. Even though my life is not anything close to what I envisioned, it's amazing in so many ways that I could never have ever imagined. For this, I am eternally grateful.

Singer Whitney Houston released a song titled, The Greatest Love of All in 1986. In this song, there is a lyric that says, "Learning to love yourself; it is the greatest love of all." She goes on in the song to sing another line that says that it is "easy to achieve." On that note (no pun intended) I have to politely disagree.

For many years I" thought" I loved myself, but as my life evolved, and as each year passed and I became older and wiser, I was slowly figuring out that I really didn't love myself the way I thought I did or that I should be. I took a good, hard look at the people and situations that were surrounding me. I knew deep in my heart they were ultimately mirrors for who I am, and in the end, it was a strong, glaring realization of how little I loved and valued myself. It was frightening, difficult, and challenging to embrace a reality that clearly showed me that I did not love or value myself the way I should.

For approximately ten years, I was consistently denying and resisting my soul's true passion and calling of being a Professional Psychic Medium. This resistance always centered around two false beliefs I held about myself. One, I was not worthy of doing the work of a Professional Psychic Medium on a full-time basis, and two, I did not love myself enough to give myself permission to take that leap of faith.

My worthiness issues and lack of self-love consistently show up in my life over and over again. They present themselves in my work life, family life, friend and romantic relationships, and even in the process of decision making. It presents itself as a constant loop of people-pleasing, having no or very limited boundaries, and putting myself last, to name a few ways. Questioning my worth and lack of self-love was everywhere. It was a way of life for me.

Once I consciously made the effort and choice to stop the insanity of jamming the round peg (or situations and people in my life) into the square hole, I slowly, with baby steps, started to learn how to love myself and understand my worth. This has taken me on a journey that I will frequently refer to as "surviving to thriving." I still continue to work on these two self-concepts each and every day. Once I began to make the conscious choice to love myself and know and realize my worth, I made a commitment to healing and loving myself on purpose. When I made that commitment to myself, my whole life changed—for the better. I chose to evolve on purpose.

Listen, no one. Absolutely no one grows up thinking or saying, "Hey, I'd like to be a Professional Psychic Medium! Where do I go to school?" For me, following my soul's passion for serving Spirit as a Psychic Medium has been an intense number of years filled with learning, understanding, and continual questioning of my worth to do this work, knowing, accepting, and truly owning my own worth and loving myself. It was part of learning and trusting the growth process with Spirit and myself. Never an easy one.

It would take more than 15 years for me to fully accept that I am a Medium and know my worth and own and accept that I am here to serve, help, guide, heal, inspire and empower others through my Mediumship and energy work. It was through the strategic placement of others in my life that I would finally begin to see the light and the path that Spirit had prepared for me in this lifetime. I slowly began to embrace my soul's purpose of who I would become and continue to evolve into each and every day. Ultimately, a professional Psychic Medium.

It was over a span of ten years of "surviving" that looked like this; working a full-time job and working a part-time spiritual business, weight gain and a weight loss journey, a failed marriage, toxic relationships that consisted of mental and emotional abuse, challenging friendships, and countless other mentally and emotionally challenging and draining situations that ultimately led to a stress-induced mental and emotional breakdown in conjunction with a worldwide pandemic. This would finally lead me to an epiphany that I was merely surviving in life and not at all thriving and that I was truly here in this incarnation to live out my soul's passion and purpose of being a professional Psychic Medium.

It took me half my life to realize, embrace and understand that I am not a victim in life and that life happens for me and not to me. During the first half of my life, I looked at it through the lens of a victim and a "poor me" attitude. I didn't fully understand that difficult people and situations were ultimately in my life to lead me to where I needed to be. I held many beliefs or stories about myself that were untrue, but I believed them anyway. My two biggest stories or beliefs center on the concept of not being worthy and not loving myself. These concepts would elicit a sense of fear, false beliefs, shame, and self-doubt within me. It was an endless loop of believing I am not good enough, comparing myself to others, "I can't," "I should," "I wish," and "I don't have," are just a few of my stories. I was gaining absolutely nothing from these self-limiting beliefs except more negative experiences on a continual basis.

We are given the beautiful gifts of "choice" and "free will" to help us embrace what our soul has come here to accomplish in the physical world. Once I started to look at life through the eyes of love and compassion, I was wide awake and realized that these people and situations in my life who brought me so much angst and turmoil were ultimately my gifts to help me grow and push me to where I am today.

It was only when I committed to healing myself that I could then replace these false stories with the feelings of love, happiness, power, and excitement. Only then could I fearlessly step into who I truly am and who I am becoming. I only understood this concept after my breakdown that left me with a breakthrough. The breakdown is ultimately what led to the breakthrough that taught me there is more to life than merely surviving and settling. For as many baby steps that I would bravely take forward on my Mediumship path, at times, I would take ten giant steps back. Learning self-love and worthiness, at times, can be brutal.

Fast forward to November 2019 when life finally begins to catch up with me and Spirit is yelling at me so loudly to leave my teaching position, but I am too afraid to take that leap from a safe, secure teaching job to one of uncertainty (my Mediumship) even though it's my ignited passion.

For ten years, I worked two jobs. By day I worked as a special education teacher, which is a demanding position. I would race home at the end of the school day, change my clothes, shove a snack down my throat, get in my car, and race to my office. I also worked weekends. For the next ten-plus years, I live my life religiously by a calendar three months in advance. Doing mundane chores such as laundry and going grocery shopping become overwhelming and stressful. There is way too much on my plate, but I was in denial. My girlfriends have to make dinner dates with me months in advance, and I feel intense stress when I have to fit in family time or other fun events on weekends because I am thinking—I have client appointments, I have weekend chores, or maybe a family or friend event. These are supposed to be fun things, not stressful. As time marches on, I can feel resentment growing and brewing inside me. I started to realize that I am truly not allowing myself to be fully present in the moment-appreciating each moment-loving each moment—being grateful for that moment because I was always ten steps ahead, thinking what was next on the to-do list or I was in an emotional state of feeling some sort of resistance or resentment because I didn't have any time for me. I was truly in survival mode, thinking about what was on the never-ending to-do list for that week, the week after that, and what responsibilities for both jobs needed to be done, and the list goes on and on and on.

It is now December of 2019. I am a very healthy person. I had a weight loss journey in my early thirties. It completely changed my life. I never went back to my old habits. Prior to 2019, I had been run down, feeling lethargic and lacking energy. I had been getting sick on and off, gaining weight, sleeping five hours or less, dealing with toxicity and drama at work, dealing with personal issues as we all do, and trying like hell to be the best special education teacher, friend, co-worker, sister, daughter, and Psychic Medium that I could be all at the same time. This is where I refer to the phrase that says "never judge a book by its cover" because the pages in between may surprise you. Each day I showed up to work dressed nice and put together and did my job, but the truth is on the inside was falling apart. I was finding it harder and harder to keep my life together. I started taking tranquilizers to help me remain focused through my work day and night. CBD oil was also my best friend to keep me calm and in the present moment as best I could. I got through Christmas. Amen.

It is now January of 2020. I have been sick for eight consecutive days. I visit my doctor, and she takes my blood pressure. It is elevated. She knows I maintain a healthy lifestyle. She asks me what else is going on. I begin to tell her all of what is happening in my life and tell her that I can't keep it together anymore, I can't focus, I am taking tranquilizers and CBD daily, and I am having difficulty being focused and productive at either job. I just can't handle it all. At this point, I am sobbing uncontrollably. She informs me that I am in the midst of a stress induced mental and emotional breakdown. She writes me out of work. No work at all. No teaching work and no spiritual work. She instructed me to keep exercising and eating right. Keep up my meditation and journaling, and that I needed a therapist ASAP.

This was a huge eye-opener for me. I don't have breakdowns. I am strong. I don't go for a few days without showering, I don't have difficulty sleeping, I don't skip meals to eat, I don't get stuck in the feeling of anxiety so much so that I am paralyzed by it and unable to function or focus on getting through my day. I got this, but the reality was, Spirit was trying to show me there was a better way to live my life and that I was clearly out of balance and denying who I was, all while keeping myself from living my passion on a full-time basis out of fear, worthiness and a lack of self-love, those old stories kept me believing that surviving was the ONLY way to live life.

During this time out of work, I didn't tell my family. I didn't want them to worry, and I personally felt I had to figure this out alone. As the days pass, it starts to become glaring and apparent that as grateful as I am to work two professions that I love, I realized I was merely surviving and not thriving. I am missing out on so much life has to offer.

Until this point, before my breakdown, I was contemplating a leave of absence from teaching for the next school year because I wanted to truly live my passion of Mediumship. I wanted to see if I was worthy of it, love myself enough to know I can and deserve to thrive and not just merely survive. The breakdown was my "no–brainer" answer. It had to be done. Without question, I applied for a leave of absence from my teaching position.

It's true. There are no coincidences or accidents. Life is divinely orchestrated and, to some extent, some of our experiences here in the physical world are preordained and cannot be changed. They are fated so to speak. We have choice and free will, and we use those "gifts" to help us navigate our fated experiences and how we will handle them in order to help our soul grow and evolve here in the physical world. I say this because it was no accident when Spirit placed a particular individual in my path in the midst of my breakdown to show me that I could most definitely leave teaching and live my passion each and every day and that I was worthy. As I look back now, this experience was definitely fated and divinely orchestrated. This individual had their own business and lived their passion each and every day. When we got to know each other better over time, I could feel and sense the freedom they had each and every day in their life while living and working their passion. I longed for that freedom. I was jealous of it. I wanted it and wanted it badly. It was shortly after this experience I began to envision what my new life could look like if I left teaching. Was I worthy of being a professional Psychic Medium? Did I love myself enough to let myself envision this passion I had? Time would tell. This individual was an angel in disguise. Most definitely a true blessing and the nudge I needed. I needed one badly.

My leave of absence was approved, and it was as if Spirit was patiently waiting for me to apply for the leave and for it to be approved because the moment my leave of absence was approved, I was blessed with so many amazing opportunities to work with other talented Psychic Mediums and develop my own workshops and classes all while taking a mastermind course to help take my business to another level. I was booking more and more clients.

It was during my breakdown when it was me, myself, and I, and my therapist (on a weekly basis) that I began to shift, grow and evolve. New routines and healing techniques helped me to begin to appreciate how special I was. I am unique, just like a snowflake or a fingerprint. I began to do more of the things I love, like take long walks outside, read more books, and reconnect with friends. I stopped comparing myself to others and focused solely on me and my journey and what my soul was yearning for. I forgave myself for being so hard and critical of me, and I forgave others for their poor choices and decisions that negatively affected my life. Forgiving others meant that I could make peace with the situation(s) and have a better understanding through the eyes of love and compassion at a higher vibrational level as to why those circumstances had to happen. I was not being nice to them by forgiving them. I was growing and evolving. All of these instances came from self-love and ultimately were shifting my consciousness to a higher vibration.

During my leave of absence, I kept up my self-care routine that I had adopted during the months of my breakdown. These new routines were uncomfortable at first, but slowly my soul grew into longing for them because they made me a better person and Medium. They raised my energy and vibration to new levels. I was going to bed early, getting up early, and reading pages from inspirational books, writing in my gratitude journal, pulling some oracle cards for my day ahead, and giving gratitude for all that I have in my life, eating good food, exercising and meditating daily. I was evolving and loving every minute of my new life.

Hindsight, in my opinion, is a true blessing in disguise. I have grown so much from it. During my breakdown, I began to reflect upon past and present situations in my personal and professional life. They started to make sense as to why they needed to happen and why they were divinely put in my path. Many missing and unsolved pieces of my life finally started to have clarity and purpose. In the end, the grieving of old people and situations began to lay the foundation of my newer, higher vibrating spiritual self. These new connections with individuals in the spiritual community eventually combined to form new partnerships, friends, contracts, and opportunities in all forms.

My new life was shaping up, and it felt invigorating, exciting, and full of good challenges and growth. I needed these people and fated situations and experiences of the past to help my soul grow, stretch, push, and ultimately help me learn who I am, where I had been, who I was evolving into and where I was headed. These reflections were sad, hard, and trying. As I was shedding who I believed I was for so many years, I was also at the beginning stages of evolving into the version of myself that I had been denying for so long. My worth begins to come into focus a little bit more, and my self-love increases slowly day by day as I embrace my new way of life, living my passion, making self-care a priority, and listening to what my soul came here to accomplish. Thus, I began to evolve on purpose. I could feel it, see it and sense it. It's sad, scary, exhilarating, and liberating all at the same time. It was looking like the comeback was going to be greater than the setback, and who knew? Who would ever think a breakdown would lead me to a life that I would absolutely love, but that is exactly what was happening! I started to love and embrace the new me, and it felt like home. It felt good. It felt real. I felt like I was finally getting it right. I found my place, my passion, and my purpose.

I became tuned in, tapped in, and turned on to the present moment during this intense time of healing, learning, self-love, and self-discovery. Spirit was stronger than ever in my life, and they taught me that through the ultimate love, the love of self that I could accept and embrace this passion of mine. This deep sense of self-love that was growing within me, helped me develop a sense of worthiness to embrace my passion on a full time basis—a beautiful shift or evolvement of self-began.

I often refer to myself as a beautiful and continuous work in progress because it's very true. My journey from surviving to thriving and breakdown to breakthrough helped me to start changing my life and re-writing old fear-based victim stories that I have been telling myself for many years. I continually work on these stories. It's a life-long process. As a result, my life has changed drastically and dramatically and for the better. For the first time ever in my life, I can honestly say I LOVE my life, and I know more than ever what it is like to love and value myself. I could never, ever say that before. Not ever.

Today, I am excited to say I don't work a job any longer. I have the absolute honor of living my soul's passion each and every day as a Professional Psychic Medium. I took the leap of faith, followed my passion, and I left teaching. At the end of the day, it's all about me. It's about knowing that I am worthy of self-love and seeing myself for who I really am—a worthy person filled with love and light.

I am slowly learning that when I accept and love myself enough to stand in my truth, in my light, in my power, and in my worth, everyone benefits, including me. When I finally embraced these beliefs about myself, I started noticing that people, opportunities, and situations that are in alignment with who I truly am started to show up in my life effortlessly. I stopped apologizing for who I am and became vulnerable, and put myself and my story out for the world to see and hear via social media and various podcasts. I learned that when I took a leap of faith, freedom, worthiness, and self-love were on the other side of fear, and it was waiting for me all along. I was worthy all along. I had to learn it, and I continue to learn it Every. Single. Day.

I am learning to open my eyes and see every situation for what it is. Not what I think it should be, what it could be, not for the potential it holds, not what my expectations think it should be or could be, but to see it for what it truly is. Feel into it. Be in the moment. Surrender to it. Place no expectations upon it. Not always easy, but I am learning.

Through my breakdown and healing, I learned to push past my fears and establish new habits and routines in my life which were once unfamiliar and uncomfortable. I had to let go of limiting beliefs and be 100% committed to creating the life and freedom I envisioned for myself. I started living my life in a more meaningful and purpose-driven way. I continued to walk away from some people and situations, grieving them and giving thanks to them for helping me grow and move forward in life. This journey is slow and continuous. At times a painful process, but I am extremely grateful.

When I embrace life through the lens of self-love and worthiness, my life becomes more meaningful and purposeful. I celebrate each day for the big and small joys it presents to me. I've learned that love of self means putting myself and my peace of mind before any drama or negativity. I've learned to look for the gift that lies within each challenging situation that presents drama or toxicity and give gratitude for them, find the silver lining, grow and learn from them and keep moving forward. I embrace where I am at in life at any given time. I am reminded that self-love and worthiness happen while I am present in each daily moment, and I tell myself I am doing an amazing job in life. I am grateful for everything big and small each and every day. When I commit to loving myself, I am more emotionally resilient, invincible, compassionate, patient, and tolerant. With this perspective, I can see situations through the eyes of love and compassion.

I continue to evolve on purpose and share my story in the hope of empowering and inspiring others to do the same. I continue to learn that the greatest gift of all is learning to love myself, and for most, it's not easy to achieve but, I am doing it! Giving myself the gift of self-love and worthiness looks and feels like happiness and gratitude each day for all that I have and for all that I am. I am grateful for all that I am becoming. I am enough. Always. I give myself permission to love myself because I am worthy and deserving of love from myself and others. I am excited and proud to continue my journey of healing people one soul at a time as a professional Psychic Medium.

ABOUT THE AUTHOR
DEBBIE SQUIZZERO

Debbie Squizzero is a gifted, evidential Psychic- Medium and spiritual healer who has a strong natural ability to connect with Spirit. Debbie is dedicated to "healing people one soul at a time." Her path has led her to enhance her gifts though focused study with many remarkable Psychic-Medium teachers and mentors. Formally, an early childhood special education teacher of 22 years, she holds a Master's Degree in special education, and is dedicated to lifelong learning and growing in any career. She strongly believes that continuing education is the cornerstone to any profession. Personal difficulties in her early thirties drew her to a reading with a local Intuitive Healer, where she discovered her spiritual gifts that would change her life. Eventually, she left her teaching career in order to follow her passion of Mediumship. Debbie encourages her clients to live successful, fulfilling lives by delivering accurate, healing and loving information during their session. Her goal is for each client to experience a positive session that will leave them with a sense of ease, peace, comfort, closure or healing. Her desire to help others comes from her own struggles in life. Those struggles have helped her grow and develop into an excellent Psychic Medium. These significant events occurred so that she could deliver messages to her clients with a deep sense of compassion and understanding for them. She loves to empower her clients with energetic practices and tools in order to help them learn, grow and heal themselves each day while navigating the challenges of their self-discovery journey while here in the physical world. Debbie lives in the small state of Rhode Island-USA. She is grateful for the love and support of her family and friends.

Website:
www.debbiesquizzero.com
Instagram:
www.instagram.com/debbie_squizzero_medium/
YouTube Channel:
www.youtube.com/channel/UC_eLTqWxDeo5V7_gsW-QG2A

5

EMMA JOHNSON
MAKING THE UNCONSCIOUS CONSCIOUS

*T*en years ago, this page would have been blank. I wouldn't have had the courage to share my story on this kind of platform. I wouldn't have felt like I had anything to say. I would have been frozen in inertia, petrified of how it would have been received and that I had done it wrong. In truth, I wouldn't have even had the opportunity because I was still living in circumstances that kept me blinkered and living on autopilot. Forty years ago, the five year old me was a happy, carefree little girl who loved playing with her friends and going out for a walk in thunderstorms.

As that little girl evolved, part of her journey was to go through disconnection, loss, betrayal, and bullying. All because she was different, sensitive. Having lost my Grandma at an early age, I carried a lot of grief for most of my life. I was never able to say goodbye because she left while I was away on a school trip. I never got to know her as an adult, and I still miss her every day. I took solace in food, and this was the start of my emotional eating challenges. Little did I know, at that point, that I was also an Empath. Instead, I went through school knowing things, sensing things, and being told I was paranoid or imagining things by those too embarrassed to admit what I knew to be true. Always on the periphery of friendship groups, I felt alone and adrift then, and I forget how it started.

I became rebellious and overcompensating. Sarcastic and self-deprecating. Better to get in first before anyone else could hurt me. As I evolved into a teenager and then went to University, the emotional comfort seeking manifested into spending money I didn't have and accepting poor treatment from unsuitable boys because I didn't have a strong enough sense of my own value and worth to receive anything better. The spending continued; subsidising and trying to buy people's love and affection. Until, at the height of my money issues, I had £50,000 of debt. Rooted in the shame I felt over not being good enough. I reached for high-end clothes, accessories, and expensive meals at nice restaurants to prove I was acceptable. I had repeatedly been told by boyfriends that I wasn't good enough and that they were leaving me for somebody better, and I didn't love myself enough at that point to have left first. For most of my life, I have lived with the good old Empath challenge of being an open book. People eagerly tell me their life stories, as if we've been friends for years. Others feel they can say literally anything to me, including their unsolicited opinions on my choice of clothes, makeup, hair, men, etc. So I flew under the radar for the longest time, and the debt and the weight crept up and up. Until 2013, when I discovered EFT, and my life truly began. Sometime in my late teens, I had received my first Reflexology session and fell head over heels in love with the feelings it brought. All the peace I had been looking for enveloped me that morning, and the fascination with Traditional Chinese Medicine continued from there. I trained in Reflexology but didn't qualify—yet another symptom of my decimated worthiness and deserving set points. I was made redundant, lost my home and my relationship on the same day, twice in four years during my twenties. But I could cope with the practical stuff, so I soldiered on. Even my bank manager called me a tough cookie. I suppose it helped that I descend from a seemingly long line of independent and feisty women who can make lemonade out of lemons. But I still didn't do anything constructive with the good chunk of redundancy money I received both times. I squandered chance after chance of finishing my Reflexology training and opening my complimentary health business. I guess I never really felt sure I could make it work. After all those years of being told I wasn't good enough and then having the "evidence" to prove it in all the losses I had faced and then, I had what I affectionately call my Holy Sh*t Moment. I had come across Emotional Freedom Techniques, or Tapping, watching a few people online; Nick and Jess Ortner, Denise Duffield Thomas, and Kim Eibrink Janssen. Again, I felt that deep, warm, contentness descend and envelop me, and for the first time in my adult life, I knew things were going to be okay. I quickly sought out a couple of courses to test it out and had good results. So good that I decided to train in it myself to be a Practitioner. I will never forget that HS moment. It was my first attempt at taking a client through a round or two of EFT. I asked her the right questions. Our eyes gently met, and on the fourth or fifth tapping point, I could literally sense that she had felt a shift. So, I began to nudge her towards the positive statements.

She paused slightly, smiled, and said quietly, "wow, you're good." At that moment, I made a choice that this was to be my future. In so doing, I collapsed all other options and committed myself fully, which I had never done before with anything. I have never found anything before or since that allows space for and creates such incredible shifts in people, including me. This was the moment I began to consciously evolve on purpose. One of my favourite quotes is by Carl Jung - "Until you make the unconscious conscious, it will direct your life and you will call it fate." That was the second HS moment, reading that quote. The third was finding out I was an Empath. You see, to me, it meant that everything I had ever believed about me not being good enough or fundamentally flawed was simply not true. It was other people's views and opinions of me. And over time, I was able to unshackle myself from them and the impact they had. The last decade has been an adventure in so many ways, and I could spend a year or more telling you about the details, except all you really need to know is this—our brain is designed to keep us safe no matter what. It scans everything today and beyond and compares it all to yesterday. If we survived yesterday, then whatever happened is deemed to be safe. And so, we can end up going through life running 90% on autopilot, doing the same things we did yesterday because they "kept us safe." It doesn't have to be that way. I changed my old stories using EFT, and my life today is a million miles from where it could have ended up. I chose to evolve on purpose, starting with uncoupling from my identity as a people pleaser. It's very common among Empaths for us to take up that mantle, and it stems from a feeling of not being fundamentally safe at the Root Chakra level. Because of that, we spend our time ensuring that everyone else is okay, their feelings are managed, and that the energy in the room feels safe.

Over the years, I have invited so many experiences into my life to allow me to people please, which now I am eternally and profoundly grateful for. The memo I got from the universe that I was finally ready to stop people pleasing was equally as epic. After having a perfect credit rating, I woke up one day to an email from a credit watch agency saying, "your credit rating is very poor." Shocked and confused, I logged into my profile, thinking something must have been incorrect. There it was in front of me, that coloured circle and a big pointer on the left-hand side, showing how disgraceful my credit now was, seemingly overnight. I won't tell you the finer detail of what had happened to get me there because I'm now in a place of total and radical forgiveness over it. Suffice to say, however, that it was the proof I needed that I had to make a new choice to evolve even further. Still on purpose. And that's exactly what I did.

In the space of 12 months, I left my corporate career, my 13-year relationship, sold the big house by the sea that I thought I needed to feel whole and complete, and moved home to be closer to family. Those markers in the fabric of time are very precious to me. Each one showing a rapid evolution, completely on purpose that would simply not have been possible without me letting go of my old stories, programming, and worthiness and deserving set points. Set points that had me on a very different trajectory to where I am now, and the best part is that it was easy, joyful even. Just as I worked through the programming and limiting beliefs I had been carrying, I also tapped in the moment so that I was able to surrender and make the perfect decision for me at that moment in time. All thanks to the process called Emotional Freedom Techniques, or Tapping. You see, when we tap on Acupressure points while recalling or being in upsetting times or thoughts, we are sending a calming signal to the Amygdala, the brain's safety centre. We also trigger the release of Dopamine and Serotonin, which relax and comfort us. Just what I had been looking for all those years ago. The best part for me is that Tapping then dissolves the neural pathways between the upsetting thought and the somatic response in the body, meaning that you can think about that thing but not be triggered by it. You can give a voice to the truth of how you really feel, instead of suppressing it and not asking for what you really want or need. You can feel safe whilst acknowledging your true feelings, instead of having to put them to one side and manage everybody else's. You can come back into your body from way up in your head and calm those spinning thoughts. You can become grounded, present, and resourceful, no matter what else is going on around you or to you.

This process is incredibly effective when used on lots of things, but in my particular story, I used it to work on my feelings of unworthiness and not being good enough. These feelings are at the root of my emotional eating and money issues, and nothing else has been able to get me the results that Tapping has on these issues. We all inherit programming from our parents or main caregivers, and we carry that forward unless and until released. The challenge here is that we don't know what we don't know. So we continue doing the same things we have always done, wanting to change and not realising that we can because it all feels so permanent. So intrinsically a part of us. Then comes the blame and the self-flagellation. I should be able to get my life together, I should be able to sort this out. We strive harder and try more and bigger things, feeling like we should know how to do everything, even the things we don't know we will need to do in order to get the goal we have set for ourselves. Talk about a recipe for failure. But still we strive. Proving our worth to others for fear they will judge us. Compensating any easy joy, money, love, or other good thing we receive with a painful counterpart. Earning the big money but making sure we are seen to be working really hard to compensate. "Wow, she earns a lot, but she works a lot of hours." Sound familiar? We also attach really huge emotional agendas to goals we set ourselves, so huge in fact, that the thing we are trying to achieve becomes the thing that gives or withholds us from finally feeling—worthy, safe, loved, whole, successful. The list goes on. If I had only known about all of this when I was in my late teens, I would have put all the pieces together and likely would not have treated money the way that I did. Or my body, for that matter. Irrespective now, however, because I believe that all roads lead to where you are. In other words, we are exactly where we are supposed to be, and everything happens FOR us as opposed to TO us. As uncomfortable as that statement can be for some, particularly when terrible things have happened, I believe with all of my heart that there is a gift and a calling in most things in this life. Whether that is to not spend another moment in regret or to create a movement to help others through the same situation we experienced. The gift for me was to experience such a deep sense of loss and separation that I knew exactly how to hold space for those still in that space. The calling for me was to create a movement to show as many people as possible how to use Emotional Freedom Techniques to feel better naturally and take control of their lives and their evolution.

I'm feeling a familiar internal sigh of relief even writing this because I know what that could mean for so many people, just as it did for me. It could mean moving from unworthy to unstoppable. From not good enough to infinitely and always enough. From stressed to calm and from held back to forging fearlessly forwards. Your past does not have to equal your future. You can evolve on purpose. And in so doing, you get to pave the way for future generations to do the same. As within, so without, and what changes in us ripples out to the collective because we are all made of the same stuff. My mission is now even bigger than the immense changes I have experienced because of this beautiful, elegant and simple mind body technique. These days, everything I do is about helping people to free themselves from the pain of the past, see how incredible they are in the present, just as they are, and forge a brilliant new future for themselves and their loved ones. To help them evolve, on purpose.

ABOUT THE AUTHOR
EMMA JOHNSON

Emma Johnson is the Founder and CEO of Inner Smile and Empowered Prosperity.

She helps Introvert / HSP Entrepreneurs stop the Shame and Sabotage cycles of Procrastination, Playing Small and Proving their worth by overworking, over giving and under earning. An Advanced Master Trainer in Emotional Freedom Technique, Emma also certifies other Trailblazer Practitioners to help spread the healing ripple further.

With a BA Hons in French and German, Emma has lived internationally for years and is now settled in North Lincolnshire with her beloved dog Boss. An avid fan of anything to do with Holistic Wellness, Emma has been studying and researching for over 30 years to bring all of her knowledge and intuition to her sessions with clients. Her purpose is to change the way we experience ourselves in this lifetime, through changing the way we deal with stress, money and our right to be here.

Instagram/Facebook @innersmilecoach
LinkedIn:
www.linkedin.com/in/emmajohnsoninnersmile/
www.empoweredprosperity.com

6

JESSICA VERRILL
EVOLVING THROUGH CONSCIOUSNESS

"*Helping* spirits, guides, angels, and the divine consciousness. I'm not ready. I don't feel ready. I have more work to do. I wanted to finish my degree, I wanted to be married first and to enjoy my wedding fully with my soon to be husband, but if this soul is here to be with me now, I will trust your wisdom, I will love him or her, and I will do my absolute best. It will all be beautiful, and I will love this baby with all of me. I surrender to what is for the highest good of all."

It was mid-fall, and I was standing in the woods looking for objects for a ceremony. I was in a weekend workshop with my beloved shamanic teacher, and I can't recall what it was on or what the ceremony was based on. What I do remember is knowing I was pregnant, I had just gotten engaged, and I still had another full year of school left to finish my bachelor's degree. I wanted to go onto graduate school, as at the time, I thought I needed more credentials and degrees to make a bigger impact on the world. And here I was, having all of my visions shaken up.

I have always wanted to be a mother. I have known that for what feels like all of my life, and I know my parenting and work with children is a huge part of my creation and purpose in this lifetime. I just wasn't sure this was the time. I also always knew I wanted to be an author, but that's another story for another day. Through all of the other fluctuations in my life, these were my True North.

The longing to have my own family was such a strong pull. It wasn't if, it was when. I also knew that I needed to have space and time to be home with my family as much as possible. What works for everyone is unique, and for myself, I wanted to be a mom. I didn't want to have to send my kids off to daycare to go work for someone else. I have never had a 9-5 job, instead creating income from self-employment, jobs with flexibility, and a higher rate of pay for shorter hours like bartending, massage therapy, coaching, and teaching classes on energy and massage.

As my entrepreneurial journey continues, I continue to create it with my value of freedom in mind. To fully be present in motherhood and running a business, there needs to be the structural aspects in place that I am able to flow within as well as having my internal aspects of self on-board and attended to—the mental, the energetic, the emotional, the subconscious.

Parenting and entrepreneurship are similar in many ways. Sometimes you think you're doing it all wrong, there's a tendency to look to outside influences to guide you, it can look like others are doing it better than you or have it all together, and it's constantly changing and prompting you to go deeper. When we are able to clear through our limiting beliefs, heal our wounds and deactivate our triggers and strengthen our energetic system, we are able to connect more into our own guidance, what works for us, and are ultimately able to be more present and connected to the beauty happening all around us. It allows us to experience more joy, love, and happiness. It's not always easy, but totally worth it.

The ultimate goal in my energetic and coaching practice has always been to help my clients connect more deeply into their internal compass or guidance system, through clearing out anything standing in its way much in the way that I have, and continue to, do so within my own life and being. It serves me hugely in conscious parenting and business—life in general, really.

The first step is to become conscious or aware of how or where you are limited/blocked/wounded.

Does the sound of a child crying trigger anger in you? Do you go into fight or flight response when you feel cornered or trapped? Perhaps it's low self-worth, intuitive blocks, people pleasing, needing to control everything, second guessing yourself, or being completely disconnected from your body. The list goes on and on. Where are you disconnected from yourself, your life, and your body? Do you tend to distract yourself with television, social media, or substances? What are you avoiding feeling? Where would your inner child like to have a voice? How do others push your buttons?

Be kind to yourself and withhold judgement. I have a thought process when I'm triggered or reactive to something or someone. *"Thank you for showing me where I still need to heal."* I mean it, if we are not able to take a deep look at ourselves on all levels, we are not able to be conscious enough to make a change. We all have our places we are stuck, and having a curious perspective can really help with the blame, guilt, and other lower frequency emotions we can get stuck in.

With awareness, everything can change.

HEALING

This is not so straightforward, and healing is definitely not linear. You may find yourself clearing out different aspects of the same incident or different aspects of a belief. It may require past life—or other lifetime, again it's not linear—work, energetic clearing, belief work, mindset shifts, or emotional purging.

Hire a coach, energetic healer, hypnotist, or psychotherapist if needed. Be discerning and be aware of not going through the same thing continuously. In my experience and in my work, it has become incredibly apparent that we do not always need to talk about things or to know the details of what we are clearing or mending in order to do so. It does not need to take years of weekly sessions to heal the trauma from being bullied. Energy and our minds work quickly if we believe they can, program them the way that we want them to work and let go of attachment to the stories.

I have seen well-meaning professionals cement in things like victim mentality, trauma consciousness, and it can keep someone stuck in a certain experience or mindset, so be discerning when allowing anyone access to your energetic system, or mind.

There's a lot that can be done on your own as we go, and the beauty of it being, the more energy we release from certain circumstances, clearing energetic debris or attachments or releasing limiting mindset beliefs, the more we bring back into ourselves. This generally helps the process continue more rapidly and allows us to have a greater connection with ourselves.

HEALING ENERGETICALLY

Our energetic systems are not something that we are typically taught about in our life. We talk about our bodies, a bit about our minds, and some of our emotions. The latter two are still being dismissed or stuffed away.

If you aren't familiar, the energetic system is a system that has the potential to create massive havoc on our lives or to fully support us. Once we learn how to connect in and utilize what I call "Energetic Hygiene" then we allow all facets of ourselves to be in flow and harmony. As things that start as energetic imbalances can develop into physical challenges, it is vital that we learn to optimize it.

One really simple and foundational piece of work I typically guide my new energy clients into, is the practice of grounding. You can find lots of great YouTube videos or articles about this, some that I have created myself, for further support. This exercise is great for bringing yourself into the present, releasing things that aren't yours (yes, we pick up energetic debris and attachments from people, places, and things), giving you stability and a base for life.

Sit or lie down with your eyes closed. Begin to take a few deep breaths, imagining that you are releasing any mental chatter, your to-do list, or any other distractions.

Focus your attention on the base of your spine, this is where the root chakra is located. As you bring your attention or mind's eye to this center, begin to imagine you have roots, a cord, or an anchor that drops or grows from this area down into the earth.

Continue to focus or imagine it going deeper and deeper, down into the center of the earth. Breathe. Connect. Feel. Be.

Begin to imagine anything not serving you—any energetic debris, attachments, energetic contracts or vows, promises, mental chatter, all being released down this cord or roots where it will be transmuted by the earth.

Sit with this for as long as feel necessary. When it feels complete, bring your attention back to your heart, connect in, breathe and bring yourself back into your body into this space and time.

For extra oomph, I LOVE doing this outside. I connect in with the healing frequencies of the earth and allow myself to match my frequency to her's. This is also great for children, and when we've left a busy place, my daughter is upset or off, I remind her to put her roots in. Ideally, you would do this multiple times a day but strive for a minimum of once per day, which can be as quick as 30 seconds as you get used to the practice.

There are tons of modalities, channeled healings, vibrational essences, and tools to help you dive in more, that I would recommend or practice myself, however, if I would recommend only one thing to help you stay centered and as a basis for your energetic practice, it would be grounding.

CONSCIOUS PARENTING

As we evolve on purpose, we are bringing this power back within us as we release them from things that generally are not serving us. As we pave the way for future generations, the more centered and calm we are, we can teach emotional regulation, offer support and be fully present in the moments that our children really need us to be. We are able to parent consciously.

Conscious parenting, to me, is the ability to parent in a way that you are conscious, or aware, of your choices, actions, and reactions instead of relying on unhealthy programming or triggers. It allows the child to grow into their own gifts, understand and have confidence in themselves as a sovereign beings, and have a stronger connection to their own internal guidance system.

It baffles me that so many children are given so little choice or control over their lives until they near adulthood, and we suddenly expect them to know themselves well enough to make long-term decisions around their future like attending university, career choices or joining the military, not to mention all of the other responsibilities that fall on one's shoulders as they reach a certain number of years in this current life.

The more parents and caregivers are able to heal, know and honor themselves, the more natural it will be for them to do to others. It is not usually the easiest decision or experience to break familial patterns, be aware of societal programming and become so tuned in with ourselves and our children to be conscious. Other times, we simply don't have a model for how this looks, what to do, how to respond differently than how we were parented, and to know the line of what is supportive structure and what is too confining. To me, this is a constant challenge I face—am I offering enough space for her to grow and trust herself, her wisdom, intuition, body, mind, and emotions but the right amount of structure for her to feel safe and secure within doing so? Am I teaching her (discipline) instead of punishing? Am I falling into the fear that she's too loud, too wild, too this, or too that?

People are constantly being told or given messages they are too this or too that. I, for one, am so incredibly sick of that narrative. Do this to be liked more, make everyone else more comfortable, dim your light, dim your happiness, dim who you are. AGGGHHHH!!! Is it no wonder that so many of us grow up with no concept of who we really are underneath all of the masks, the people pleasing, and the programs? We don't know what brings us joy, we don't know how to be happy, we don't know how to celebrate, speak up, own our worth, accept compliments, be comfortable with ourselves, or a myriad of other things. If we don't know how to do these things, how can we teach someone else? And, knowing how this has the potential to seriously derail so much of our lives, why would we subject our children to these same patterns?

My goal as a mother has always been to respect my child as her individual self, understanding that she will have wants and needs that are different—and often—opposing to mine. It is not my job to mold her, train her, get her to comply, train her to follow directions, listen without talking back, but to ask questions, lots of questions all the time, to trust herself, to follow what she believes in, to be able to debate and negotiate, to speak up for herself, to be loud and happy, to express her emotions regardless of who and how it makes others uncomfortable. Our jobs are not to become dim expressions of who we are to fit in, to follow the status quo, or to avoid risking making someone else feel bad at the beauty of our light. It is to own our light, to shine it so strongly within, that it cannot help but radiate our to impact others. We need the light of ourselves and of others to shine upon us to help illuminate the areas where we still need healing, the areas of ourselves we have buried. The traits and characteristics within us that are the most uncomfortable for others, are very often the exact thing that is our strongest gift or asset.

For most of my life, I was called opinionated, as I had an intense sense of comprehending the injustices and imbalances in the world and wanted to educate others to make change. I could not understand how anyone could know about things such as child and human trafficking with its link to the pornography industry, factory farming, environmental issues, poverty, the theme of adult dominion over children, and so many others, and not give a fuck enough to make changes. I always felt like a rebel speaking out and against things, questioning so much of the status quo, and wanting to make a massive impact in the world. Over time, it dimmed. I put masks on. I became a people pleaser. And it was awful. I felt like a shell of who I was, who I am. Eventually, I realized that my opinions, rage, and deep need for change, was not something that I needed to hide, but that I needed to embrace. I understood that the intensity of my feelings, was fuel for my mission here, in this lifetime and existence. I don't think like other people do, I don't act like them or live my life like them, and I'm not here to. I'm here to create change, to help shift systems that aren't serving most of us, while creating ones that will.

I don't want my daughter or all of the other children in the world to need decades of healing, deprogramming, and rebuilding themselves so they can realize their potential and power. It is in all of us, and as adults, we have a duty to preserve it within all of the children in the depth and capacity we are able. I have a check in for myself when I'm not sure how to react or am feeling triggered as a caregiver: I imagine the exact scenario with my daughter and translate it to that of an adult. So, I imagine the adult equivalent, and then I ask myself how I would respond if that situation involved my husband or a friend. How would I react to an adult in my life that I love, doing something similar? That practice guides me to supporting her as a person, switching my perspective, and breaking myself out of those child-rearing patterns that I don't wish to pass along to her. This is why it's called conscious parenting. It takes work to be aware, and it's a constant practice, but one I believe is worth infinite times the effort in the impact on our children now, their future, and the future of our world.

CHANNELED MESSAGE

As a channel, much of what comes through me is working from my higher self and spiritual guidance team. However, I got the message to consciously channel in a message and transmission for this.

"All in one. We look for something or someone to be everything in one for us, and that is placing undue expectations upon that being. We do this with our children when we expect them to be good at math, reading, science, and that thing that they love. We force them into learning how we wish them to behave, act, think and feel. By doing so, we restrict their ability to experience life on their terms and what they came here to do. Instead, evolve. You are no longer living in caves, and you did not come this far to be chained to your work, your devices, or substances. Free yourself to become whole. Dare to think differently, act differently, and step out of the status quo. Trust your child and her inherent wisdom. Trust yourself and the child that is within you. She is wanting to come out. Allow her to have a voice and watch your life transform into more joy, fun, and happiness. This is the point of life after all. Enjoyment."

ABOUT THE AUTHOR

Jessica Verrill is an energetic alchemist, intuitive channel and USA Today Bestselling Author. As the founder of House of Indigo, a multimedia publishing company, she supports spiritual leaders in sharing their unique gifts and teachings to elevate their authority.

Her skills as an intuitive coach and energetic alchemist supports high levels of growth and alignment, while working directly as a channel to her personal guides. As a life-long learner, she is often immersed in books and classes, including all aspects of herbalism and flower essences, health, wellness and personal development, spirituality, and enhanced psychic development.

Jessica lives in Maine with her husband, daughter, black lab and cat —a new addition to her family that showed up in the yard. She loves gardening, communing with nature spirits, hiking, exploring nature, being around water, traveling and personal development.

publishing@jessverrill.com
Websites: jessverrill.com, house-indigo.com
FB Page:
www.facebook.com/HouseOfIndigoPublishing
FB Group:
www.facebook.com/groups/indigoinitiative/
Instagram: @Jess.Verrill
Clubhouse: @JessVerrill

7

KALI J. WALTERS
LAST TRAIN OUT, FIRST STEP FORWARD

I would have never thought ten years ago that I would be sitting here typing this out today and stepping into this person I had always wanted to become.

When I first saw this book title, I knew I had to be here because I had something to tell, but just like my first multi-author book, I didn't know exactly what it would be about; I just knew it was something I needed to share.

So I turned to the universe and really asked for guidance in this space. What is it that I am to share? What will be that piece that shows up for that one person that needs my words today? Whenever today is.

When I thought about the evolution of who I was, who I had been, and who I am today it struck me, I had to share the defining point... That one piece that changed the course of my life because it was that piece that allowed me to start evolving from the path I had been on to a whole new path that allowed me to be my highest version, something that shifted the course into creating generational change.

My thoughts took me back to that time in my life where everything I knew life to be like was about to be interrupted for the better. They took me to ten years ago...

To a time when I looked a lot differently—there was no glow, no spark, and little ambition to life. To be honest, I was in a space where I never thought that I would get out of it, so F it all, let's just drown my sorrows in drugs to pretend that life was normal...

Yep, that's right, the person you see now was once a drug addict, and I was that addict that would take 98% of drugs just to escape the reality that I had created for myself.

It's amazing, really, when we look at who we were versus who we become, and what we think won't make such a difference in our lives impacts it greater than anything else...

That's exactly what happened here. See, when I was a lot younger, say 9 or 10, I had the firm belief that I would never use drugs or be a smoker of anything. I had the ideals that even though some days there was pain in my life. At that age, I still clung to "things were going to get better," not worse, and that life would be a breeze. If I didn't think like that, my world would have been rocked a hell of a lot earlier than it truly was, but that's a story for another book, another chapter, another journey...

It was only the next year that I first picked up the drug I started on—speed—readily available in my own home. It seemed like it fixed everyone else's problems; maybe it could help mine too. The innocent thoughts of a child misplaced, confused, and just wanting things to be okay.

It's ironic really that so many people who are evolving start with journeys like this, but alas, I digress again...

That space on purpose may be digressing from interestingly enough because I'm able to share so much of my journey, but here, writing it out, it's such a different feeling...

So my evolving journey really began the day I said it... I'm going to rehab. Well, I was nudged gently, forced brutally, and given the chance to go to rehab by the actions I'd taken to get me there. To be honest, when I made the choice at first, on a conscious level, I didn't believe it would be the end of my drug usage... Not truly, it was a vacation from my using... Whatever that means.

My then partner and I started looking for rehabs that took couples because we wanted to do this process together, it would strengthen us, or so we thought. So here we are at the payphone ringing up place after place until we had it narrowed to just two places... One being the space we ended up Karralika.

Now Karralika isn't just any rehab it's one that has a carefully laid out strategy and has the greatest results because of it.

I remember sending all our details over and getting accepted. We had our entry dates, and everything worked out. My partner would be the one who would go in through detox first to make the leap, and we would meet each other in the rehab.

That was the plan anyway, and this is where nudges started to happen—my intuition waking up after a long slumber. But I was still so out of tune with her that I ignored her. For that, I'm sorry my dear intuition, you definitely knew best but, imagine where we would be if we had of taken that path...

The plan went the way it was meant to until a phone call... "babe, I've been kicked out. I'm going to be coming home." Oh shit. I had no idea why this happened, but at first, I assumed he'd taken something in with him. It wouldn't have been the first time, and looking back now probably wouldn't have been his last time. But no! This was because he "apparently" was caught with a female. Notice how I said that apparently—yeah, we'll get to that one.

So in detox that's slightly frowned upon and out he was kicked and back home he came. Well, at first, I was in the space of oh well, that was a fun game while it lasted now what? But we found ways to swap our entry dates, and I was in a much shorter time frame bussed off to detox myself—quite off my face if I do say so myself on that first day.

Things get a little blurry here. Detox was a wonderful half way space that was meant to give you a gentle way off whatever thing had you. For me, I made sure that I over exaggerated how much of everything I was on, nearly tripling how much I was using by the paperwork I filled out. Needless to say, they looked at me like I shouldn't be alive because, well, even with the normal consumption of my drugs (which by now had escalated to everything except morphine), I was an experienced user, let's just put it that way.

So detox became a bit of a blur until the night that broke me. The night where I listened hard to my body's needs for the first time in about 10 years... Yup, 10 years of using from the little age of 11 to nearly 21... I heard her crying, I heard her pain, I felt it all and felt the pain I'd been burying for all those years suddenly visible to me again.

My first true night without anything in so many years to mask it all. This became my true calling to evolve, and finally, it became on purpose rather than just running on fight or flight mode constantly. On this night, I had the cold shivers, hot flushes, and was throwing up —purging so much. I couldn't sleep most of the night, and my body just was removing all it needed for the next leg of this journey.

This night was the night between detox and rehab, staying in Sydney and with a friend at the time who was keeping me safe for the night. Yet the next morning began my first test, the test to see whether I was truly ready to evolve... to find the next level and to take the leap into listening.

That fateful morning for most doesn't seem like much, but for the 20 year old girl I was, it was scary. I realised as I opened my eyes the next morning that I was taking a journey into the unknown and that this day was the day where I truly was going to start fresh, breaking free. And as I got my suitcase ready, made sure I was dressed, and had everything I needed, I saw the minutes tick down on the clock. It was almost time to catch the train from Sydney to freedom... also known as Canberra in this case for me.

The problem? Because like in most heroines journeys, there is a problem that must be faced first, and that problem came in my friend not waking in time. And me... Me making the choice NOT to establish that request that we needed to go sooner. So I let it be, and she woke up, with 15 minutes to get from her place to the train station.

As we pulled up, I jumped out of the car, grabbed my shit, and away I raced to see the back end of a train pulling out of the station when I hit the platform that would take me away... to my freedom. I literally sunk to my knees. I was alone and terrified that I'd lost my chance to change my life as that train sped away. Not knowing what else to do, I rang my then partner and sobbed on the phone to him still kneeling on that platform... And as I spoke with him, the next train pulled into the platform, and it was the one to test me... The one that would be my choice to freedom, or back to the life I knew so well.

The train was paused, and time stood still for me as I had to decide where I was heading and what exactly it was that would become of me. That moment something inside my mind said NO, we are NOT going back!!

I hung up and looked around, still scared, still fighting the unknown but also knowing to trust deeply that something would be available that this would not be how my story ended. Not this time! As I looked around, I found the bus ticket office attached to the outside of the train station. This would be my way out if and only if there was that bus to get there.

Synchronicities happened here, as I started to head to the office, a bus pulled in, and it was heading to none other than Canberra—my freedom. The bus looked packed, though, and my next fear kicked in...

Will there be a seat available for me. I raced over there...

Now at this point, you're probably wondering why this is such a crucial moment; well, hang in there, and you'll see my reasons why...

As I raced over there, I, in a panicky shaky voice ask was there a space available for me. At first, the ticket office tells me no, nothing is available... I start to become weak, and in this moment, all the words fall out...

"I need to be on that bus. I'm going to rehab, and if I don't get there, I'm lost. I can't do this life anymore. I need to change, and this is my ticket to freedom." And in my mind, I spoke to source, begging to have my back that I need this and no matter what, I'm going to follow through. I saw in those split seconds a piece of me I hadn't seen for so long, the piece that had hope in life, the piece that loved life that wanted to live.

I don't know if it was that they felt sorry for me or if it was me throwing my energy into it. I do know that I committed to something and saw the new version I wanted to be there and then. And in that moment he said, I can fit you on, there has been a cancellation, but we have to do this fast it leaves in 1 minute!

And as I stepped onto that bus, I felt held so held for the first time in my life. By something I didn't realise I had, strength and courage.

I took the leap because I had such belief that it had to work, that I could make it work and that I was worthy of making it work. I knew that I was being divinely guided by the source in my life at that time.

This was my moment, my time to evolve, to know that there was more to me and that I had purpose again in life.

See, the problem became my greatest gift in life. If I didn't have this moment, there wouldn't have been that choice, that moment where I truly was taking on my next level in my journey and fully walking the walk to being in a moment of power for myself.

And that evolution gave me the power, the compassion, and the moment to be able to keep making choices guided by the inner knowing... Intuition. That moment when I was stuck between going home and moving forward, the choices of a different path was my key point.

From here, I've moved forward, and it's been a journey from there to coming home fully into self by keeping on hearing the yeses, the no's, and the nudges from the soul callings in my world.

I was seeing that when I fight it that things get mucky, and things become a struggle. It's all been guiding me back home, and as I allow myself to be guided through my soul and my learnings, it's that moment of sharing this.

Hear your voice, your inner voice, that one that calls you home. It's scary, and it may seem like it's so unclear why it is happening for you, it even might seem cliché to say this, *Everything happens for a reason...* I know I thought it to be cliché. There's a sense, though, when we are faced with trials, no matter how big or small, that it's always happening for us to grow and expand from. To evolve from.

The evolution of choosing to listen to that voice and keep pushing through has led me to being a mother to multiple little beings. It has led me into a space of complete compassion for all those around me.

It has led me to being a facilitator of ceremonies for women, specifically moon ceremonies, which was something that came through my journey understanding the moon cycles, and maybe this is a big part of my journey of evolving as I did that came later but just as significantly.

Through my yeses and my no's, I found guidance through the moons. The cycles are so linked to us, especially us feminine beings, with our own inner moon cycles. Becoming aware of what is happening as each piece cycles around...

Our dark moon, the new moon, is beautiful for planting new seeds to grow from—a reset if you will. One that gives us the ability to dream bigger visions and set new intentions for the month ahead...

Our beautiful full moon, reaping the rewards from what we set in the dark moon, releasing expectations, letting go of what may be holding strong, and causing mischief for us.

Knowing these things and allowing myself to dive into this spiritual world and bringing it to life here, gave me new space to see the world and connect with others, sharing this passion. Finding purpose and giving grace in my life as we all follow the ebbs and flows.

Our moon cycles and our intuition lead us, guide us, share the evolution process with us. Once we allow it to be seen, we hear the whispers of the soul and create the choice within ourselves.

These are my gifts to you to use and hear beyond your external voice —to connect with others and be guided divinely when truly in touch with yourself.

For me, this all led me to creating a movement for other mothers that are stuck in the space they are to help them hear the nudges of their soul. This movement has become The Mummas Permission Movement, and together we gather in ceremony by the moon. I facilitate these and give that space for us all to hear what is next for us our next step. I combine this with my business that allows us to be our most abundant selves without sacrificing time or freedom.

It's interesting the path, how it evolved from simply wanting out of the life I was stuck in, to becoming a way forward for me, for my family, and for those who see me. Mothers otherwise lost. Families unconnected. All these beautiful souls creating new pathways, new journeys, and evolving on purpose so that those who come after us are no longer burdened with the pain that we were gifted to shift through.

It's all there for you, and when you're ready to evolve or take that next step. Listen, and for the mother out there feeling trapped and not knowing what it could be, I invite you to come into The Mummas Permission Movement, and find your nudge forward, come join us through the ceremony under the moon, find the release. See your next step. Understand deeper what this cycle means for you.

And most of all, enjoy the journey to Evolve.

ABOUT THE AUTHOR
KALI J. WALTERS

After living a life of abuse and trauma in her childhood, Kali J fell into the state of addiction and repeating cycles she saw before her. Kali J though, found her way out of it all, by saying enough was enough and creating differently in her life.

Now Kali J is a mother to five, but more than that, she is embracing all parts of her wild, free, fun, and adventurous spirit that had been squashed years ago. Kali J now uses her story and journey to be the permission slip for other mummas to move from the role to their truth.

Kali J is now the international bestselling author of the unconventional motherhood book 'F motherhood and is the founder of The Mummas Permission Movement, which shows other mummas that no matter where you are in your world, it's never too late to create the life you truly desire.

Kali J holds to her heart moon cycles, cacao ceremonies specifically designed for women to come together as a village.

Kali J would love to have you connect with her at:
Website: kalijwalters.com
Facebook: www.facebook.com/KaliJWalters55
Facebook group:
www.facebook.com/groups/mpmovement/

8

KARE

LOSING KEN, FINDING KARE

One morning, you wake up and find out your whole world has changed. At least, that's what happened to me.

On the afternoon of August 16, 2008, I was enjoying a local fair in St. Charles, Missouri, near my home. My two daughters, husband, and I were having family time on that warm Saturday. We strolled the craft booths and admired the handmade items. We came across a business which made plaster molds of your hands. The idea of creating a permanent plaster cast of hands to display intrigued me. I thought it was so unique. Out of the blue, I thought of one of my siblings and just how cool he would think this was. I got the urge to call him in Michigan. I remember thinking, "I've got to call Kenny when I get home. He would love to hear about this!" I was excited about both making a cast of my hand and calling my brother to share this interesting experience with. Even though I had the urge to call Ken, I never did make that phone call. Of course, I did not know that it would have been the last conversation I had with my brother on Earth.

That night, I had a mystical dream. I can remember it well. It was different from many of my typical dreams. This one was not in full color but in hues of black, white, and grays. A white mist was present in my dream and surrounded the images I saw. There was a chariot driven by a wild-eyed man with his long hair blowing in the wind. The driver was swerving around corners and charging at a mighty speed. The inside of the vehicle seemed to be bursting with people. Their expressions were uncertain, and they appeared a bit frightened. The road was tree-lined and winding. There were no buildings, street lights, or traffic signals. The passengers were desperately trying to hold on and remain inside the chariot's carriage. The carriage was bumping up and down and swinging from side-to-side as it careened down the road. The driver kept on going at the same speed, despite the tumultuous ride. He did not stop or slow down. The vehicle careened around a corner and disappeared.

The next morning, my husband delivered the news to me. While I slept, my brother died in the early morning hours of August 17, 2008, in a car accident. Ken had friends who regularly took a golf trip together. It was a kind of guy's trip. They had all gone to a local drinking establishment and were heading home when the driver lost control of the vehicle. My brother was fatally injured and was the only passenger ejected from the vehicle. Fortunately, the other three people survived, including the driver.

When I saw my brother's golf buddies at the funeral, the dream I had made perfect sense. I had that déjà vu feeling. I got goosebumps! The driver of the car from the accident had grown his hair out. It was long and uncannily similar to the hair of the driver of the carriage in my dream. They had been Up North in Michigan, where dirt roads and tree-lined streets are typical scenery. The dream was real.

I have grieved people in my life, including grandparents, aunts, uncles, and even a same-aged cousin, but nothing prepared me for losing a sibling. My husband relayed the news as tenderly as possible. Both his face and voice were somber. His look and tone were an omen. It felt as though a one-hundred-pound weight was dropped on my chest. There were no words. It was hard to breathe. This was grief. I was numb.

At this point in my life, until August 17, 2008, I had recognized my psychic abilities. I used them as many of us do, listening to that voice in our head or intuition. I took heed of my "senses" and trusted that gut feeling most of the time. I used my "knowing" and really began to trust my instincts. This unfortunate event would propel me on a metaphysical healing and learning journey. I would evolve on purpose.

Many of my childhood memories are typical. There were loud and fun family gatherings for holidays. We had family vacations, mainly to Tennessee to visit relatives or Up North in Michigan. But some memories include the unpleasant times when my father's alcoholism took control of him. His wrath was felt by the people he loved the most, his family. Dad became physically abusive to my mother throughout his drunken rages. We had visits from the local police department but things were different back then. The police did not intervene as they do today. They did not take my father away. Instead, they declared our situation a "family matter."

Through the years, there were several things I remember that may not be typical for most people to experience. To me, these things were normal. Sometimes, I "knew" things. I'm not exactly sure how this happened but, I would just "know" something. For example, I had this ominous feeling about a neighbor down the street. I got the overwhelming "knowing" feeling that he died. It turns out that feeling was accurate. Usually, this feeling or claircognizance is undeniable for me. It has gotten stronger through the years, and I know to pay attention to it. I feel that sometimes I am being prepared to handle a situation when it presents itself, as in the case of the monster dream.

Precognitive dreams have been a part of my life. I had a repetitive one for years as a young teenager. It repeated itself and mildly changed over time. It reminds me of the movie "Groundhog's Day."

The same thing happened over and over in my dream, and I learned how to best escape the circumstance. The dream was of a monster coming after me. My route was typically the same. I went through a house to a set of stairs, then up the stairs, and to an attic room. The monster's face was never revealed to me in the dream. It changed over time from a dark shadow to the face of Frankenstein. The situation once upstairs was always the same. I was in fear and knew I had to figure a way out. Sometimes, I hid and tried to make myself small in the darkness. That never seemed to work. The monster always found me. The fear I had was so real. Gratefully, I always woke up before he could "get" me. I devised ways to get out of this scenario in the dream over time. Finally, I figured out how to successfully escape. What finally worked to get away in my dream was to distract the monster. Then, I would run back down the stairs to safety. This escape was rehearsed in my dreams several times over the course of the next few years. I never understood what the dreams were about. I did not realize these repetitive, practice dreams would bring me through a similar scenario. Until one day, I encountered the real-life Frankenstein and used the actions rehearsed in the dreams to escape unharmed.

My first visit from Spirit was when I was about 16 years old. Life was sometimes tough through those high school years. Things were changing, and the end of my regular school routine was looming. I had major life decisions to make. I thought it might just be easier to leave this physical existence and move to the Spirit realm. I wasn't creating an exit plan for myself but asked Spirit to take me from the physical realm soon. I prayed and asked if it could be time for me to join the heavens. The answer I received was a physical visit from Spirit. I was woken up that night to find a white mist hovering above my bed. There was a light surrounding it. It had a luminescence about it which made it unique. I was sure I was surrounded by the essence of Pure Love. A feeling of safety and calmness encompassed me from the inside out. The mist constantly moved and changed-swirling and fluid. The images of beings took shape. It was an Angel behind two small children. No audible sound was made, but I could "hear" them in my mind and knew these were my children. The Angel encouraged the children to kiss my forehead and cheek, one at a time. This filled me with love and purpose. After this experience, I don't remember asking to die in my sleep again. I had found Purpose. I knew these children would be in my life. I knew I would feel that same overwhelming amount of Pure Love. I feel that Love now with my two precious daughters. I am grateful for this experience.

My thirst for knowledge of the Metaphysical began early. In about the 6th grade I started to read books on metaphysical topics. There was a limited selection back then. I read books on ESP, Psychics, Channeling, etc. I read whatever I could find. Shirley MacLaine and Sylvia Browne's books lined my shelves. I can remember reading about Edgar Cayce and Nostradamus. There were many people and topics to explore. I relished watching the television show "Crossing Over with John Edward." It was amazing and provided proof of the Afterlife.

After the death of my brother, I was seeking tangible evidence of the Afterlife. I needed to be sure that what I "knew" was real. There is an Afterlife. I needed to reassure myself of what I had read and learned so far. Things happen for a reason, don't they? I had long believed this. There are no coincidences.

Up to this point in my life, I only had a few psychic readings done on myself. From what I remember, they were all at least partly accurate. One of the psychics predicted I would marry a man from the military. These were not the typical men I was attracted to, so at the time, I paid little attention to it. However, five years later, I moved to Las Vegas to pursue my teaching career and met my future husband. He was in the Air Force stationed at Nellis Air Force Base in Las Vegas. The prediction was accurate after all! As part of dealing with my grief, I sought out a few psychics and mediums for readings. They provided healing and guidance for me. I left feeling better, and the healing began. I was able to reassure myself of the existence of the Afterlife. I knew it was there.

My brother visited me in dreams. They were so vivid. They were not ordinary dreams. I would wake up and write them down, afraid I'd lose them from my memory. However, I have found these visits and precognitive dreams stick with you over time. Ken was able to take me to where he exists. It's a world of iridescent color and sound. It's Peace and Beauty. When I reacted as surprised to these surroundings, Ken repeated to me, "You know this place." He was right. I knew I was familiar with this place. I could *feel* it but not remember it. There are no words to describe the whole experience.

One of the psychics I went to for a reading offered a class in tarot cards. She told me that I, too, had psychic abilities. I heard this at each reading I had ever had. I signed up for the class. It was through this class and the ones that followed where my focus became directed. I enjoyed this adventure and learning about the Spirit World. The connections with fellow Seekers and Spirit urged me to learn more. I took classes for Pendulum Reading, Palm Reading, Animal Communication, and Runes. I continued to practice the skills.

I regularly used Tarot cards and began to read for others. I was encouraged when people confirmed the accuracy of the readings. In one reading, I spoke to the client about a baby. She denied the baby, and the reading did not seem to connect with her. I gave her my business card and asked her to reach out if the information made sense in the future. Several days later, I received an email confirming the accuracy of the reading. An unexpected pregnancy had been revealed in the family. I am grateful and humbled when I receive confirmation from a client. Even though I know the information does not originate with me, I am humbled and grateful that it is allowed to flow through me.

The local community college offered classes that were not geared toward a degree for adult learners. You could learn to use computer programs, weave baskets, take yoga, etc. There was a class offered in developing your psychic ability. I could not believe it! I signed up for this class, and it was an amazing experience for me. This class introduced me to Remote Viewing and built my confidence. The exercises strengthened my psychic abilities and gave me a safe place to practice with others. My psychic senses and Remote Viewing skills were proven strong. Confirmation from classmates and the skilled teacher solidified my destiny. I could feel the healing taking place as I continued to learn and grow.

An opportunity to take a Reiki class presented itself. I wanted to learn more about energy healing. Reiki enhanced my psychic abilities even further and showed me yet another avenue in the metaphysical world. On the first day of class, I remember seeing a symbol in my mind's eye around the room. I thought it was the familiar dollar sign or a treble clef. As people introduced themselves, I waited to hear that someone was a musician or involved in finance. I knew I would just "know" who the symbol belonged to. However, that did not happen. It wasn't until later in the day that the meaning of the image I saw was revealed. I learned that in Reiki there are special symbols. One of these symbols I recognized was the image I saw in my mind's eye. It did resemble both the treble clef and the dollar sign. But I had not learned the Reiki symbol yet, so it was not available through my memory. The instructor reported she had drawn them all over the room with her finger and intuitive intention. You could not really "see" the drawings with your typical vision. I was using my clairvoyance. Reiki proved to be a natural skill for me, and I embraced it. Putting your hands above someone and feeling the energy move was exciting for me. I loved the feel of the energy flow and the versatility of Reiki. I had long believed there was healing power in the hands. I learned about this method, its history, and many uses. I decided I would practice Reiki and offer it to others.

Continuing my education in the metaphysical world, I looked for even more classes. I did well on the Remote Viewing activities in the psychic development class and wanted to learn more. I found a class that was taught by a well-known former psychic for the US military. This class offered skill building in the psychic arena but was specifically geared toward Remote Viewing skills. The feedback and practice were priceless. I can remember an exercise where the teacher went to a location for us to "view." My RV session notes included "looking down from an upper level" and "a banister to hold." It turns out he was on the upper level of his deck and at one point holding the railing, looking downwards into his yard. The feedback was positive. I felt competent and confirmed in my abilities and development. This class gave me a great foundation and built my confidence even further.

I have continued to learn and grow. I have added Shamanism and Mediumship to my skill set. Each of these builds my psychic abilities more. I am forever a learner and a teacher. The Shaman path was and is, tremendously healing. I enjoy the simplicity of the Elements, and the opportunity it has provided me to heal myself and others. Shaman must go on their own healing journey as part of the process. This was profoundly healing and sacred to me.

Mediumship training has provided me the ability to communicate with Loved Ones in Spirit. When this unfolded for me, my world shifted. My brother, Ken, showed up several times in different readings, encouraging my development. He became more accessible and part of my Spirit Team. The knowledge of the existence of the Afterlife was once again proven undeniable to me. I have done many readings now, both in gallery-style and privately. During a private reading, I saw the character Archie Bunker from the television show "All In The Family." I relayed this image to the client, who confirmed the family actively compared the person in Spirit to that character! I have brought through a variety of loved ones, including mothers, fathers, grandmothers, grandfathers, sisters, brothers, aunts, uncles, friends, children, and even pets! Yes, pets are there too! Often mannerisms, personality traits, or other identifiable characteristics come through for the client to recognize. Other times personal descriptions, cause of death, significant age, or some other notable item identifies the Spirit for the Sitter. While I can't control who comes through in a mediumship reading, the client usually gets the message and comfort they seek. Thank you, Spirit!

In 2015, I opened a business out of my home offering Reiki sessions and classes. The business quickly grew to offer Tarot Card Readings, Shaman Work, and Mediumship Readings. I have participated in many events, including psychic fairs, group gallery readings, and private parties. These experiences have enriched my life through the connections with others. I am a people person. I am grateful for the thousands of Tarot Card Readings, Mediumship, Shaman, Remote Viewing, and Reiki sessions I have been honored to provide. It amazes me still. Every skill in the metaphysical world still holds me in awe. The love felt in the Spirit Realm is indescribable. There is a peace and wholeness to look forward to after this physical life is finished.

After teaching for decades, I retired and now dedicate more time to my metaphysical business, Kare Reiki. In recent years, it has evolved to include online services. I offer classes from a variety of topics, including psychic development, Reiki, mentoring, and more. I host a Metaphysical Book Club and Coffee with Kare, an informal discussion forum.

There are no time or distance limits in the metaphysical world. That is the reason readings and sessions can be held through telephone calls and the internet. In person events are still enjoyable to me, but with technology, I can reach literally anyone in the world. I can reach you! I love the feeling of connecting with others and the love from Spirit. I believe anyone can develop skills in the metaphysical area. I am grateful that past students have enjoyed the classes they have taken with me. I am honored to share this learning experience. Once again, it is humbling to be a part of someone else's healing and metaphysical skill-building journey.

Now, for certain, I know where my brother, Ken, is. I am grateful for his assistance on my metaphysical journey. He has accompanied me on this path. I know I can reach him psychically through dreams and more. My belief in the Spirit World is unwavering. I am continually learning and growing. I feel like I am where I am supposed to be. Each teacher I have come across has helped me to grow and heal. It is my desire to do the same for others, for you.

After losing my brother Ken in physical life, I have found my true self. The weight from my chest is gone. I can breathe. I am speaking my truth.

With Love,
Kare

ABOUT THE AUTHOR
KARE

Kare is a Psychic Medium and Reiki Master Teacher who grew up in the suburbs of Detroit, Michigan. She has lived in Las Vegas, Nevada and currently resides in St. Louis, Missouri. Kare has a Master's Degree in Education and recently retired from teaching. She is now working full time in the metaphysical field. In 2015, Kare established Kare Reiki, a business offering Reiki sessions and classes. Her business has grown and along with Reiki, now includes Psychic Readings, Tarot Card Readings, Mediumship Readings, and Shaman Energy Healing. Kare offers classes and one-on-one sessions, small group, and large group events. Kare has experienced psychic phenomena since she was a young girl. She often had precognitive dreams and the sense of "knowing" things. As a teenager, she experienced her first "physical" Spirit visit. In her early 20s, she learned to read Turkish coffee from a friend's Yugoslavian Aunt. Kare experienced electronic disturbances and accepted these as "normal." It was not until her brother's unexpected physical death that she decided to develop her natural skills and further explore the metaphysical field. Being a lifelong learner, and teaching others, brings her joy. Kare has read about, explored, and studied many metaphysical topics over the past 40+ years. These have included Psychic Development, Mediumship, Reiki, Remote Viewing, and Shamanism. She is an avid reader and hosts a Metaphysical Book Club online. Kare believes all people are capable of tapping into their intuition and is honored to assist those who seek to strengthen their metaphysical abilities. She is continually amazed and in awe of the Universe and its never-ending signs and synchronicities. She believes there are no coincidences but does believe in Divine Timing. You are reading this for a reason!

Facebook: Kare Reiki
www.facebook.com/reikiandtarotcardreadings
www.karereiki.com

9

KATY BAYNES
SOUL TO HUMAN COHERENCE

*A*ll we truly want in life is to be free in our true nature. To be completely ourselves and loved deeply for it. To belong without needing to compromise our essence. To never be misunderstood and seen for our pure intentions. But unfortunately, this often isn't the way.

We're born right into our true nature, perfectly curated energies and genes imprinted upon us and chosen carefully by our souls with a particular mission in mind for this lifetime. Strengths, gifts, wisdom, and weak points are all balanced in a certain way to lead us into the lessons required for our ultimate growth and expansion in this life.

But from such a young age, in our prime years for wiring the brain and heart, we are pulled from that true nature. Our free expression dulled to be more digestible by the masses, our sensitive emotions smothered in unhelpful coping mechanisms, our playfulness managed through structure, and our curiosity dampened by rules.

We're pushed, and we're pulled until we fit into a nice, predictable little box, ready to please the majority of society. Our soul is pushed all the way to the back of our consciousness. The mind is given full power. Intuition is overpowered by a need for logic and decisions that make sense over what feels good and right. But how do we feel inside? Detached, lost, lacking, heavy, restrained, in an almost constant state of dis-ease.

The cycle of life then becomes a process of the universe presenting you with lesson upon lesson, in the hopes you'll see your true nature clearly again.

An uphill battle, a constant stream of resistance, everything feels hard. Life becomes this way because you're not in alignment with who you came here to be. And the universe will show you over and over again until you notice until that little voice inside gets loud enough to know something *has* to shift. That there must be more. The purpose seeker in you ignites.

Or until the body responds in pain, ailment, or illness. You know you have bigger things to do in this life. There must be ease for you, and there must be true happiness.

And, of course, there is. You're not here to be in a constant state of struggle. Learning and expansion through discomfort and resistance, yes, but struggle and misery? Absolutely not.

See, when you're being exactly who you came here to be, ease is at the forefront. Because you're not pushing against the natural flow of your energy and essence, you're gliding along with it gracefully and in full trust of where it leads you. You are at one with your intuition, in a constant but beautiful dance between ego chatter and soul whispers.

I found human design in a time of transformation in my life. I was 28 years into a life of suppression of my true nature, expression, and truth. Battling against the people pleaser in me, being the one who can't implement boundaries, and constantly dishonoring myself.

I had been healing deeply for a few years, since the birth of my daughter in 2016, which was the greatest catalyst to my healing journey. My own mother wounds were deep.

Becoming a mother stripped me to my core and lit a fire within me to ensure my daughter had a really different experience from what I had growing up. I wanted her to know love, freedom, fun, and adventure.

I wanted her to know she was perfect as she was, and the world would move to make way for her to shine. I wanted her to grow knowing her genius and to feel safe and proud of it.

But in order to do that, I knew I needed to heal the darkest parts of myself. I had to commit to becoming the best version of myself possible in order to give her that life.

I was born into a long line of suppressed souls and dampened spirits, particularly through my matrilineal lines. I arrived here, in this body, with the mission to hold and eventually transmute the unresolved and unhealed patterns of my family lines.

I'm the line in the sand, the circuit breaker, and in turn, the outcast of my family.

Hence the inability for a long time to use boundaries, as they'd often left me abandoned in the past.

I would spend my early years having my spirit broken in many ways, not realising it was so I could put it back together again later down the track, in a new way. A fresh template, never seen before. Often before a big change happens, things need to get messy and chaotic first. Whole foundations need to crumble. We see this play out in many ways of life: the old saying "It'll get worse before it gets better" rings true here. Landing into this life and this family as the one who will change the patterns and heal for the ancestors who came before me and the generations yet to come means I arrived into the absolute chaos. The breaking point, to the cycle. I suppose I took one for the team, though my siblings sure carried the weight alongside me.

In my human design chart, my soul's imprint, I have a lot of open and undefined energy centers—7 out of the 9 in fact.

What does that mean if you don't know human design?

Your open centers are the centers you're really here to experience life in the full spectrum through. You're here to get wise through those centers, but we get wise through experience. We get wise through pain, learning, struggle, and then being able to see clearly into ourselves. Being able to alchemize our experiences and pain into pure wisdom.

We get wise because we had to go through something big, and we came out the other side more true. More fortified. More knowing of ourselves.

Your undefined centers are open and sensitive to the world around you. They're receptive to the thoughts, emotions, energies, and opinions of others, and so, this is where we look when we are ready to journey through our deconditioning. We take on conditioning through these centers every day, and so as a sensitive child arriving into a reasonably broken and narcissistic family dynamic, I took on a lot.

My childhood felt chaotic, hard, painful, toxic, traumatic. I don't doubt I was loved, but the expression of that love felt so conditional and rigid I retreated as far into my own inner world as possible. I learned to soothe and support myself, and I learned how I was expected to show up in order to try and keep the peace and fit the image my family had in mind for us all.

Those years couldn't have been more damaging to my spirit. I became wired with beliefs that I was never good enough, no matter what I did. That love was so conditional based on meeting the expectations of another. That my worthiness in this life balanced on how well I could follow the orders in front of me, even when it didn't seem fair or make sense.

That I could only experience connection, and be celebrated in my struggles, never my success. That I was unsafe, and my safety didn't matter to the people around me.

That my emotions were not a true representation of my experience and didn't have a safe place to be explored and expressed.

Drama queen and hypochondriac were the labels given to me often when I was expressing my truth. I learned how to shrink away, how to numb myself, and how to become completely malleable to the situation I was in. Keeping the peace in order to protect my heart became my work as a child, and as the years went by, I moved further and further away from who I truly am inside—knowing now that I am so deeply sensitive, and that is one of my superpowers. I realise I couldn't have been further away from my true spirit in those years.

I believe the frequency of a child is so pure in those first years. Unhealed, reactive adults cannot match the frequency of a child and nurture them from a place of peace and neutrality. So the child adapts and learns to drop their own frequency to match the environment that they're in—prioritising the comfort of the other over themselves. Although it doesn't feel good inside, you receive external validation for meeting the expectations of your family and assume, as a child, it's the right thing to do.

The clever thing about children is that they'll still find a way to honor their design as best as possible, though. And I often got myself into situations where I could be in nature and with animals, which became my medicine. I got to clear out my centers and my aura and become myself again in these moments.

My magic, my savior during some of my toughest years, was my horse. Shadow.

How symbolic our meeting was. I found him neglected in a paddock at the end of my street. He was unwell, unloved, and alone. Which, at the time, was exactly how I felt.

Everybody told me I should put him down, but something in me ignited, and I fought for him. It was the first time in my life I would hold my ground and fight for something important to me. The little rebel inside me was awoken at this time.

Horses are such beautiful, spiritually connected creatures. They demand a relationship of trust, communication, and depth. They reflect your own state back at you in each moment through their body language and reactions to your intentions and actions. I nurtured Shadow from my spirit, and he nurtured me right back.

In the winter, I would sneak out of my bedroom window in the early hours of the morning to take him hot oats for breakfast. I remember so fondly, standing in his frosty horse paddock. My back on his chest, his head resting on my shoulder. Whiskers tickling my cheek, and his breath in my ear. He would breathe life into me for that day, and I would return home to go numb again. Get myself into autopilot, and tick boxes until the afternoon when I could see him again.

I learned unconditional love for the first time, and I learned freedom, fun, play, and joy.

I had a purpose, to look after this creature. I didn't realise how much he looked after me too.

I couldn't feel my own heartbeat, but I could feel him. And it was enough.

I could feel so whole and peaceful in the hours I spent out in the horse paddock, my aura clear of anything low frequency. I was deep in purpose at that time.

As a teenager, in reflection now understanding how I'm energetically wired to interact with the world around me and process energy and emotions, I can see how the secondary schooling system was never going to support me. I didn't fit anywhere and found the hundreds of people, noise, and constant need to be 'on' exhausting.

My body was already responding to the constant state of stress and survival I'd been in for years, and my mental health was weighing me down a lot. I had anxiety attacks daily and entered a really murky depressive episode for two years of my early teen years.

Suppressing all of the big and messy emotions became harder and harder, so I numbed myself with drugs and alcohol, further depleting my spirit. Physical dis-ease was showing up in my body, such loud and urgent messaging coming through my body for me to change something in my life.My body was begging me to heal the trauma it carried, but I wouldn't understand those messages until a little later in my journey.

If we can understand that we are all here in complete individuality, with intricate ways, we're designed to exist here. Sacred gifts that are just ours, embedded in us to shine brightly simply by being our truest self. The natural way we desire to show up, speak, work, flow with our inner energy is the exact way we are supposed to do it. We would be so much more free, we would be so much more understanding of one another, and we would have worlds set up to allow people to enter them and exist in them; however it feels good to do so.

My healing journey really ignited in my early twenties, beginning actually with my physical body. The messages from it became too big to ignore. I gave up on the western health system I felt like was trapping me and returned to plant medicine. I say returned because it felt like such an innate, resonant way of responding to the issues I was having in my body. Fuelled by the desire to overcome infertility and have a child, I nourished myself back into health.

I got really curious about the mind, body, and spirit connection and started really noticing myself in all areas of my life. That curiosity led me down a path of reading hundreds of radical remission stories and realising that every single one of them had an energetic and emotional component to their healing journeys. This was another deeply resonant topic for me to explore, my whole body would respond to what I was learning, and I knew I had to dive deeper.

I was beginning to have times in my life that felt good, peaceful, happy. Although I was still seeking true happiness outside of myself often, despite living in one of the most beautiful places on earth (Wanaka, New Zealand) and having an incredible husband, great jobs, and wonderful friends. There was always something missing, something I was seeking.

I was still playing out a lot of the stories I had on repeat within, the ones I had created to survive my childhood. And initially, I was still intertwined in my family's energy, further feeding my internal narrative.

I fortified the decision to estrange from them fully after my daughter was born, and it was only once I was really out of those cycles I could heal on a much deeper level. The universe was still delivering me the same lessons over and over again, the ones in which I lost myself in— where I dishonored myself. Where I was the people pleaser, keeping the peace for the sake of never being challenged or having to navigate confrontation. I was terrified of confrontation, had no confidence to speak up for myself, and lacked the courage to stand strong in myself every day.

Over time my self-awareness became more and more refined. I was able to take some self-responsibility for myself and my life. I started to notice myself and how I responded to situations—how I responded to particular types of people. What sort of things triggered me. The experiences in which my heart would lock itself into a cage, protecting me.

For a long time, I just noticed, observing myself each day. The things that stood out the loudest I began to journal, and I would start to be able to link that reaction to something from my childhood. Recognising another time in my life, I had felt that way before, and I realised that although I was being triggered in the moment, it was the suppressed emotion and the story playing out because of it that really needed the healing. I got to rewire my entire self and rewrite all of my stories.

Seeing the reaction, tuning in to where it was rooted within me, feeling all of the emotions, practicing acceptance and forgiveness, choosing a new story. Over and over, I followed this strategy.

This process of constant observation and responding to myself was around two years long. But as I released the layers, thought cycles, and stories, I became lighter and lighter. I began to know little parts of who I truly am; I could feel it. Without this noisy weight of the rest of the world taking up space in my inner land, I could hear myself. In the way I mothered my baby, in the moments of challenge where I could open my heart for a few seconds longer, in the inspiration and creativity that returned to my vessel. I had dreams and a deep sense of a much bigger purpose.

I shared some of my story with a good friend once, and she said to me, "Surely you can't have been through all of this for no reason. You have to share your wisdom with people, you have you show them there's a way through the darkness" and that lit a little candle in my core. My story had to be for something, and it had to mean something.

And so began the spiritual awakening.

I began to practice stillness in hopes of soothing this forever busy and noisy mind of mine. I have open head centers, so I've learned to love and appreciate my busy mind. It's a work of art in there when I can slow it down just enough to really acknowledge the inspiration and ideas within. My nervous system didn't know how to cope with stillness. It didn't feel safe. In fact, years later now it still takes me 15 minutes of soothing myself to get into a relaxed state for meditation. This was a big part of why I deepened my breathwork practice. I had found my breath during my teen years as I was soothing myself through anxiety attacks and realised how powerful it could be to breathe. To bring in relaxation, calm, and remind myself I was alive. But during these years of my deeper healing and seeing into myself, I was able to use my breath to see clearer. To connect to myself on a deeper level and expand my consciousness.

I always encourage kindness to the self if you struggle with stillness too, for some of us who have carried stress in the body for a long time, it's not as easy as sitting down cross-legged and switching off the mind. My work was just sitting with the mind and watching the thought cycles moving through, creating the time and space to process things trapped in there.

I noticed a lot of the continuous thought loops I couldn't switch off were conversations and interactions I'd already had in the days, weeks, and sometimes months prior. They still remained because they were situations where I still wasn't being true to myself. Where I'd left things unsaid, boundaries crossed, and unresolved emotions remained. I expanded this practice into sitting still in nature, feeling the breeze and temperature of the air on my skin. Listening to the noises around me, noticing all of the little bugs playing their part in the world. This practice really connected me back into mother earth and the oneness of all. And that frequency landed me a whole lot more appreciation and love for myself and my role in this world.

I started working with energy healers, I bought my first oracle card deck, and my journaling became more channeling messages of wisdom and magic rather than always unpacking my shady past. And, I invested in a human design reading.

I had no idea what human design was, but I was intrigued. The chakra system was a part of my daily practice by now, so I was drawn in with that and my interest in astrology.

I certainly didn't expect to sit in front of a stranger who could see into me better than I'd ever been able to see into myself.

It was a complete relief to know I wasn't broken. To know the parts of me I'd always been shamed for, and made wrong for, were perfectly me. I had all of this open energy and could feel into others on a really deep level. That, as a projector, I was here to guide people, the collective.

Human design isn't this modality that trumps your own inner knowing or replaces the need to still heal mind, body, spirit. Energetically, emotionally, humanly. It's not a fix, it's a part of the journey. It's not learning *new* things about yourself, as opposed to realising the exact parts of you often dulled or avoided are your most potent parts. It's bringing language, empowerment, and awareness into the parts of yourself that long to shine but didn't know they were allowed. It's highlighting the traits within you that you've struggled to accept all of this time and further feeding the expression of the parts you know are your truest nature.

You get to look into the imprint your soul chose for your human and realise that it all makes sense. That struggling to keep up with the world around you is true. That your big, explosive emotions that some days feel bigger than you are true. That your desire to pivot, change your mind, and reroute more than people can keep up with, is true. And as you work with your design, noticing where it already shows up in your life, whether that's the beautiful expression of energy or the shadow of it, you get to further refine yourself.

You can see into the centers that hold the stories of your past and figure out which ones are truly yours and which aren't. Your chart provides you with a map through yourself, and you get to explore it simply through living. I booked multiple human design readings. I loved everyone's unique take on it and the different expressions of my design depending on what they could see into.

And the further I connected into my true essence, the more profoundly I could see the areas I was still struggling to hold my own energy. I could stand in a confrontation and notice when my open emotional center was picking up big feelings that weren't mine and when my open heart was making them mean I wasn't worthy. I could feel my open identity center beginning to wobble as I was challenged on my very being and my open head centers taking opinions on as if they were my own. And with that level of awareness, it meant I could learn to navigate these situations ahead of time in a way I knew would nourish my energy. I would spend time each morning connecting into my own centers and energy through meditation and breath, making sure I knew how I was really feeling before I ventured out into the world.

And I was tested, over and over. I got a little stronger each time, remembering the dampened spirit of little me. Who thought the only way was to dissolve and let the other take up all the space. I dug in a little deeper each time, in honor of her.

I gave myself permission to use boundaries, to walk away when I felt confused about if I was still in my own essence or had become the other, to clear out my energy and return.

I gave myself permission to have hard conversations through writing, so I could say everything that needed to be said before getting swept off into emotions that weren't mine.

And I began to lean into the parts of me that felt so true and so magical. The deep, mystical parts. The parts that love to retreat and sit in my own company. The parts that could take chunks out of my own story and recraft them into beauty to share with the world.

I learned that my gifts were in the deepest crevices of myself and that my life should flow with ease.

Finding my purpose wasn't about figuring out what I was supposed to do as a job or this tangible thing I was supposed to be doing. It was just a journey of coming back to myself, a rebecoming. It was hearing that little voice inside saying, do this, be this, show up like this today and choosing to listen to it. Being in my purpose is just being me, fully. No matter what is challenging me, no matter who can't understand me.

Human design and my own healing and awareness gave me an relatable tool I could use to see where to go next, based on what the universe was presenting me at any given moment.

I would say almost every person I read for asks for direction and purpose. And every single time, that can only be found by journeying into the depths of yourself. Calling out the suppressed versions of you, longing to be felt and expressed in this world. Giving them their power back. Letting them shine. And now I sit, more fortified in myself than ever before. And from this place, I get to guide others back into themselves. What an honor this life is!

Giving other souls those same permission slips that shifted my world, to say you get to show up however it feels good. And in fact, the world, maybe now more than ever, really *needs* you to show up that way.

Through human design, breath, ceremonies, and guided journeys.

Connecting humans back into their souls, their intuition, and their hearts.

Soul to human coherence.

ABOUT THE AUTHOR
KATY BAYNES

Deep and mystical, a guide to soul coherence, creator of sacred experiences and landing magic through words. Katy has a mission in this life to guide people into the depths of themselves, to connect deeper to their truth, soul and intuition. To hold space for healing and self-mastery. She is currently creating experiences through Human Design exploration and readings, Women's Circles, and ceremonies, guided breathwork and sacred group portals.

Every experience Katy crafts is ceremonial, safe and potent. Built on connection to self, expression and self-exploration. She doesn't like to play in the shallows, but arrives in the deepest, most sacred parts of you and your story. That's where all of the magic lies.

Katy is so honored to be a part of this beautiful co-creation, sharing a little snippet of her story in the hopes it gives someone the insight and guidance they need. To realise how perfectly curated you are for this life, and how through rebecoming who you were always supposed to be can bring you into the most nourishing, grounded, connected and abundant life possible, with ease and flow at the forefront.

Our fields can dance together through these channels:
Website: www.katybaynes.com
Instagram: www.instagram.com/katy.baynes/

KELLY BAYE
CHALLENGE IS GROWTH

*M*y father always took me to the library as a kid—I won a contest once for all the books I read. My big brother & my father meant the World to me.

My father joined the military as a young man. I didn't understand his job, and he didn't talk about it. My brother was the coolest guy! A sun-streaked blonde surfer who went to Burning Man, surfed in Australia, knew people from everywhere, made me mix tapes of funky music, & ate exotic foods. He led the way into living an authentic, spiritually driven life.

At 19, I got my first Oracle card deck.

I'd work shifts till 1 or 2AM, and after I'd watch movies, eat pizza and drink diet pop. I received a diagnosis of IBS. My father dealt daily with the effects of Crohn's disease, so I was under the impression such digestive susceptibility 'ran in the family'.

I also received a diagnosis of depression. The young doctor told me "diet & exercise"—I didn't understand what he meant.

At one point, I checked myself into the psych ward. I met a girl there; she believed what they told her about herself instead of finding her own truth through her pain.

In that moment, a deep knowing of *my own truth* was stirred within me: *I'm not going to find the answers I'm looking for here.*

The answers would come, though, no surprise, in a book!

I found one on *Natural Alternatives* to various Health issues; I opened to a section on **Homeopathy**—something I had never heard of before! I had a strong sense that *I will find answers here!*

It seemed mundane—yet was pivotal! The empowering sense of taking responsibility for my own experience—my own Evolution! There was a whole world of answers and potentially even something guiding me to these answers!

My friend told me she knew this guy who was just like me! No one had *ever* said that to me before, so naturally, I was intrigued!

He was a cool older guy; he captained his own boat, had five blue-eyed Huskies (that went *everywhere* with him) he played the guitar & sang—like my father—but songs my brother knew! Needless to say, we connected instantly.

To me, he was an underdog; recently out of the hospital, he survived not only a pancreatic attack but a ruptured appendix too—the worst the doctor had ever seen!

I always rooted for the underdog. Life had been hard on them; they just needed to be shown there was still love in this world for them... *Right!?*

It wasn't long before we were living together and after reading a book all about it, I was pregnant with our first child!

I still believe *Love is the way*, truly *the only way*, though there are deeper truths to this too.

Such as, other people's love is not enough.

You need to love yourself and develop the ultimate relationship between you and your *Source*.

Acknowledge and be *Thankful* for the Blessings that surround you daily.

Be as loving as you can, in as many ways as possible, which includes undoubtedly loving yourself.

The macrocosm reflects the microcosm.

Coming to realize you want more, or better than, what you once were willing to accept is ok! That is, in fact, the Evolution of your Soul.

I left everyone and everything I had ever known and moved across the country during the 7th month of my first pregnancy. We drove a 1979 Champion *propane* motorhome from Vancouver Island, British Columbia "back home" to Cape Breton Island, Nova Scotia, where his parents lived. A 60 hour drive took us 26 'daze'; prevalent in B.C. travelling east, the accessibility of vehicle propane dwindled.

My father, my wonderful Pa, took me travelling to foreign and exotic places! We had first-hand experience of Rome, Athens, and Cairo! We sailed down the Nile, visited famous ancient temples, and enjoyed Life in Greece while he was stationed at the Embassy. We also journeyed to Turkey, took a train to the former Yugoslavia, and ferried out to various Greek Isles. Another time Syria & Israel—each mind-blowing and expansive opportunities I Am forever Thankful for!

Needless to say, a month-long *honeymoon* trip across the country, 3rd trimester pregnant, four Husky dogs (plus one cremated in the back), dragging all my worldly possessions, completely trusting in this guy, venturing into the unknowns of the big wide-world and motherhood, was *not* ranked my favourite trip ever.

We moved a kilometre off the road to a little cabin in the woods— totally new for me! Not long after, two of our dogs were shot. They had been mistaken for wild animals—these dogs were our children before we had children. One with his back split open by the bullet miraculously made his way home, needing many stitches. The other was found, thrown down an embankment, his collar removed. He was *the* sweetest dog ever, soft face, laid-back personality; he'd hide his toys under a blanket...

An ominous sign, perhaps. I was often alone while he'd work til dark or be catching up with old friends. Left with only him to vent to, along with my hormonally induced fluctuating emotions, that he wasn't prepared to deal with—things took some difficult turns early on.

I gave birth at 22, and our less than healthy dynamic grew, along with our first son.

I can see now how it must have been hard for him. I realize all of the things he must have been going through: becoming a new father, being *back home*, old unhealed wounds, new responsibilities, old and new expectations—I see it now; back then, my own suffering was paramount in my experience, which, unfortunately, he seemed more capable of adding to rather than alleviating.

During my second pregnancy, I looked into dream interpretation; my dreams were never more vivid than during pregnancy. This search led me to the *University of Metaphysical Sciences* (UMS). It had everything I was looking for and more! I was soon enrolled.

I learned my baby was in a breech position, yet my reading and research confirmed I presented no other risk factors. I was determined to avoid any unnecessary medical interventions. After all, breech babies were born safely. I was young, healthy, this wasn't my first, and as I would learn, there are plenty of Natural/Alternative options to support and/or remedy such situations. People have turned to these solutions for centuries—millennia even - things like herbs, acupressure & *Homeopathy*.

Here was my open door!

I took a deep dive into Natural and Alternative Health options! After all, with my studies from UMS, I was working on my Soul, it only made sense to study the Body & Mind as well, right?! I was inspired by a book whose author supported people Spiritually yet understood the aspects of Body and Mind along with the interplay between all aspects!

This resonated deeply as my path! I would find my complimentary school, *the Vancouver Island College of Natural Wellness* -my plan was set!

Through UMS, I was reawakened to the Truth of our Spiritual Essence—*We are Spiritual Beings having a Human Experience.* I wanted to support others Soul, Body & Mind including my unborn baby, his father, and even my own father—who was not only suffering from Crohns' but diabetes now too.

I knew I needed some healing too—now I had a bigger reason than just me to dive deep.

I met with a Homeopath in the city—she reminded me completely of my mother; her clothes, hairstyle, manner. I hadn't seen any of my family since leaving on our *epic* journey. My mother had not agreed with my choice. What my mother wanted for me did not resonate as *my truth*.

I had been reading about Homeopathy, learning to help myself. The Universe chuckled when this Homeopath, a doppelganger of my mother, told me the remedy I needed was not the one *my own* research was telling me I needed.

Reading *The Food Revolution* by **John Robbins**, as part of my course materials, impacted me profoundly. After reading it, I no longer drank cow's milk, we fasted from meat for a few months, and the microwave went—never to be seen again.

A lot of my thoughts and beliefs may have seemed "too much" for him, especially being *back home*, around people he'd known all his life. My ideas were seemingly "out there". I was a West Coast, granola-eating, hippy chick with all these "backwards" ways and ideas.

Maybe my notions challenged his belief systems. Maybe he didn't want some of it to be true because once I delved into understanding the toxins in our air, water, food, things we expose ourselves to, and all the ways the system intentionally damages us -keeping us sick for their own benefit- it all became quite overwhelmingly clear! Especially when he would consider his own lifetime of exposure and now needing to keep our babies safe! This required research, awareness, and calculated choices; cognitive dissonance, stress, and times of conflict loomed large.

He was also now tasked with building a home for us. In 2006 he cleared the land and laid the foundation for our new home. It should have been a celebration, but it wasn't. He would be gone well past nightfall, leaving me pregnant, alone with a toddler. We had as many dogs as ever, even puppies, along with the added pressure of me now having goals for myself with the degree programs I was pursuing. Clearly, I needed some support, but there was none.

I would look to him for support since he was my only physical connection with the outside world, but he was unable to find compassion or empathy for me after coming home from a long day of physical labour. Unable to get what we needed from each other, things erupted into trauma on this occasion and others.

What was I to do?

I wanted to be Thankful for the incredible opportunity of building our own home. I would look to the cards to try to understand how to make things better; was I on the right path? What choices could I make knowing I could only change myself? Could I find the right Homeopathic remedies that would help shed negative aspects, like the peeling of an onion? The stress in our relationship hummed in the background when it wasn't the focus of the moment.

He would credit me with helping him make changes that allowed for a reprieve of pancreatic attacks for many years and began to share in some of my 'preachings'. Some of it he appeared to truly embrace; he stopped drinking cow's milk too.

I continued to study and use Homeopathy for anything and everything that came up. My understanding was that even if I didn't get the exact right remedy I was always strengthening our Vital Force -by providing Homeopathy for my family at all! This is why I love Homeopathy! All bumps, bruises, black eyes, split lips or any other traumas endured, could be supported and potentially healed on multiple levels, with Homeopathy.

I didn't feel he was looking to grow or focus on self improvement, after all he had a family to care for - mouths to feed! It was a whole new experience for him too; his family once believed he would not have any children; I think he believed it too...before he met me. I believed as long as he took the remedies I offered his evolution and healing would be assured.

He was a good dad; he loved the children, was there for them and always made sure they had full bellies. He taught us to love the woods, how to take the bones out of fish in one piece, and the love of Classic Rock. His physical health & unresolved traumas needed attention but he put all that aside to show his love by working hard to build our home -his legacy.

Things got more difficult when a divide was created over having the children choose a favourite parent, instead of us being united. Our parenting styles were different and there were some fundamental misalignments we never seemed able to reconcile.

I was the mother of his children and that meant something, but respect had been lost. Things were said and done that sunder a relationship; it's difficult to love yourself after accepting a relationship on such terms.

I wanted to *feel* different in what I thought was supposed to be *the* most important relationship in my Life; I knew if I could do that then things would be different.

The foundation complete, he then got to work building our house. I was pregnant with our third child. I believed that a child was a Blessing on our union. January 2007 I gave birth to our third son. The New Year's baby -less than an hour after entering the world, along with me (fresh outta labour) and the rest of our beautiful lil' family - made the front page of the local newspaper!

The circle of Life became evident that year when his grandfather would lead the way to the Other Side. The only grandfather I had known, Great Papa's Life and death impacted many including his grandson. After the funeral his Aunt, a mother of 7, would remark about our child, "There's something wrong with that boy".

Our second son, who had turned from his breech position a week before he was born, Thanks to Homeopathy, Acupressure & an inverted position, would receive a diagnosis of Autism.

A year later, my Pa visited! He spent more time travelling than we got to spend together, but perhaps that's typical...? He tried to check into the local motel we were staying at. It was off season and our house was still in various stages of construction that made living there difficult. My father had incredibly honed in on exactly where I was! He met his 3 young grandsons & got to see the house that would soon be ready for us.

My brother would come out too! Visiting friends in the city he made the three hour drive north. We toasted the power being turned on in our new home and I made him dinner, while he played with his nephews and the dogs. I am so Thankful for both these visits!

Joyfully, I completed my goal, earning my Bachelor's of Metaphysical Sciences degree! I rewarded myself with a trip to Toronto; I was going to a Hay House event! I had learned of **Louise Hay** & her incredible work, _You Can Heal Your Life_, due to a reoccurring injury. Not only had her book impacted me profoundly but so did another Hay House author, **Sylvia Browne**. I read all of her books, deeply taking in what she shared about the Other Side, Past Lives and the Meaning of our Existence. I broke into tears as I stood in front of her to have my book signed; it wasn't until I returned home that I realized, perhaps my fatigue, increased emotions and new found appreciation for East Indian food might have something to do with me being pregnant.

Not long after our daughter was born, an Oil & Gas company wanted to buy land down the road from our home. This company planned to drill and frack in our rural residential area right next to the biggest freshwater lake in the province, allowing for any run-off to contaminate the lake!! There was no way we could let this happen - Big Business and industry polluters in our neighbourhood!?! Our water, air, peace, way of life and our children's future were all in danger! The external threat gave us something to come together on, it even helped grow and strengthen our community ties, despite the tensions.

Finding the Blessings within the traumas was becoming a more accessible way of navigating all the hard times, a perspective I Am Thankful for, and one that continues to serve me.

I had been using my cards all along; learned meditation, even experienced Past Life regression in order to understand my current relationship difficulties. I had found refuge in Nature, with the stroller and the dogs. I took a Reiki course, figuring I would go deeper – once I learned distance Reiki I could help my father! I was also working to receive my designation as a Nutritional Consultant and Master Herbalist, since finishing my Bachelors.

There were still difficult times. I went to a transition house more than anyone should, but there were things worth trying for - our kids, our home and the future!

Then the World as I had always known it ended.

It was June when the call came. They told me my father was dying in the hospital. This was the first I'd heard of him even being in the hospital! By the time they called me he was no longer able to speak. I asked them to put the phone to his ear.

I said, "Pa I love you, I will watch for you in Spirit."

From reading Sylvia Browne, I knew I had to let him know not to hold on for me.

My father continued attending church even after the rest of us declined. I knew he was curious about all the wonders he believed the afterlife held. He'd had a beautiful life - a lovely family, seen the world, and served people for many years as someone who believed in a Higher Power. Life had offered him all he needed to experience. I wanted him to know that I held Faith in his continued existence after this human experience.

The Reiki Principles provided solace; I would do self-treatments throughout the trip for my Pa's funeral. I recognized how he still provided loving gifts even in his death, such as his most prolific gift - the gift of travel. I traveled for his funeral back to see my family, whom I had not visited for nearly ten years.

A year after my father left this plane of existence my world would be shattered again.

The call I received this time was that my beloved brother was missing.

He'd gone for a personal retreat into a National Park, to mark the one year anniversary of the passing of our father, and no one had heard from him since.

Devastated, I took my card deck as far into the woods as I could go. When I asked the question then drew the reply, all cards came up *Singers* -Energetic Essences in our Earthly experience. In all the years I had been using this deck I had never drawn all *Singers*.

I knew my brother was now also in Spirit.

I believed if anyone would communicate with me from the Other Side my father and brother would! I had been finding dimes since my Pa transitioned; I had read previously coins were a sign from Spirit. I also read if I wanted a sign all I had to do was ask, so I said out loud, "If I keep finding dimes Pa, then I'll know it's you!"

I heard a psychic medium would be at a local venue -I had to go - maybe he could tell me about my brother! The news would come before the event that his body was found. I still went. To a crowded room the psychic said, "...I'm picking up dimes..." Mind-blown I exclaimed, "That's me!" He spoke of my father sending me small change, of my mother losing a child and more that resonated on a conscious and subconscious level, providing comfort, confirmation and reassurance.

It was 2012 and I took my brother's passing to be the world ending event that had been predicted. The world changing on our own personal levels like we'd never known before sounded far more manageable than the unimaginable disruptions that loomed eminent.

After all, a Loving Source wouldn't let all that was, end, right!? Not support us, hear our prayers of gratitude for our difficult but beautiful lives and our beseeching prayers of guidance..?

A Loving God and Goddess wouldn't have the world end, not now, not after once again, blessing our union...right!?

December 21st, 2012 passed gently. The following spring, at seven month gestation I gave birth to our Spirit baby.

God's Grace, he looked just like all my other babies... Clearly after this, I felt Source was telling me something different than ever before about the state of our union.

I ended up leaving. I got my own place & lived there for 3 years; I figured if I was the problem, here was the opportunity for him to do better without me.

I got a job, my own vehicle and somewhere along the way I learned the profound truth, *As a Soul I am never really hurt.*

He was in our Lives regularly. His grandmother and father both joined the Spirit World the first year we lived apart. They died within days of each other; both were deeply significant to him.

I was able to feel differently about him; in my own space, he felt like a *new guy*!

I was writing my Master's Thesis, had received my Reiki Master attunement and completed my Nutritional Consultant designation.

My lease ending, along with other events, led to us all moving back with him, into the house that was nearly complete.

There were dreams of us building a business at this home that still seemed worth pursuing. I loved this land and the home built with his blood, sweat & both our tears; a place I *came home* to more than anywhere else my entire life. It wasn't long though before the old patterns played out in typical fashion; depression crept out from recessed places.

His back pain was chronic; there were other pains too, along with consistent stress and grief -the enduring Hard Knock Life of the Underdog.

I decided my own Truth was that I was ready to Live Life focusing my attention on what I wanted to experience, how I wanted to feel and acknowledging a Loving Source that is always supporting me all along the way. All I had to do was remain open and receptive to that Truth. The Law of Attraction, manifesting, Feng Shui and a deep favourite Ester Hicks & Abraham were lighting the path forward for me. He didn't want to listen; he was doing his own research. He'd heard my 'preachings' all along and found the info to confirm what he was sensing within.

His worst fears would be realized; he received a diagnosis of pancreatic and liver cancer.

He'd experienced people receiving this diagnosis growing up. His expectations may have already been set, but I still appreciate his willingness to test my teachings. Choosing against extensive conventional treatments, he was optimistic about all the options I assured him we could work with - Accupressure, everything organic, juicing, Essiac, wheatgrass, supplementing and more!

We went over his blood-work with the doctors who said "get your affairs in order". They monitored specific numbers significant to his liver; the tools we employed influenced these numbers in the direction they said would indicate improvement. Then apparently those numbers didn't matter anymore, they reiterated he was dying.

Perhaps, that was the most *humane* thing to do. Perhaps they were utilizing the nocebo effect or perhaps they knew what to expect because while he declined chemo or radiation he took the pain medications prescribed all along. I understood the pain of pancreatic cancer is the worst pain there is, so I couldn't blame him, but I couldn't give up either. I know he loved me because of all the things he was willing to try, but also because he asked me to marry him.

I was with him, when six months after his diagnosis, he took his final breath.

Knowing, '*As a Soul I Am never really hurt*' helped me immensely throughout his illness. I had a card deck called *Talking to Heaven,* I got after my brother passed that had remained unused - I turned to it immediately and received much solace.

I knew I would be ok because Source doesn't give us anything we can't handle, right!? I had survived my World crashing like the Tower previously, and I was still ok.

He had been seeing a Naturopath daily, she saw the Healing Environment I was creating for him with Essential Oils, Gems, Healing Frequencies and Reiki. She shared a love of meditation, and would introduce me to Bioenergetic feed-back & *Certified Pure Therapeutic Grade* Essential Oils (CPTG EOs).

After his passing I went deeper. Completing my Master's of Metaphysical Science, attaining my Master Herbalist designation and becoming a dōTERRA Wellness Advocate. dōTERRA's CPTG Essential Oils and supplements could have been another potent tool for him, but now Thankfully, they serve me and my children; favs include blends like Console, Forgive, Peace, Adaptiv and Cheer!

I came to understand that just like my Pa, he offered gifts even in his passing. Gifts like the community our beautiful children and I turned to, the wonderful home he built for us, the incredible people I met along our journey together, the tools I could rely on that I had been cultivating the entire time and the incredible direction my Life was now taking because of all we went through.

Recently our Autistic son, who loves music, played a song I wasn't familiar with, but the message resonated clearly:

"Those were the times
That was our life
I probably wouldn't change
One little thing if I tried
Moments together mapped out
Like stars in the sky
Now you're in the things that I do

Still I miss talking to you..."

I Am Thankful for the roles he played in this Lifetime. I Am Thankful for all my Life is, because we travelled this journey together. I know he is happy now in ways like never before and free of all suffering. I know he is with us and I look forward to receiving more messages and guidance from him, any and all Past Loved Ones, along with the many benevolent Energies that root for all us underdogs, calling us towards our Best Lives Ever!

Recently I earned my Holistic Health Practitioners designation and experienced the unbelievable feeling of having Source work through me to help a friend fulfill her life-long dream of becoming a mother! I'm gaining more tools and skills every day, expanding my business and joyfully serving those whom Source brings into my world. I Am truly Thankful for this Glorious Life & look forward to what's to come!

I wonder, *how can Life possibly get any better than this!?*

ABOUT THE AUTHOR
KELLY BAYE

Kelly lives with her four children & three dogs, on a beautiful slice of Unceded Mi'kmaq Territory in Northern Nova Scotia, Canada.

A PhD. candidate, Kelly holds a Masters degree in Metaphysical Science, is a certified Holistic Health Practioner, Reiki Master, Ho'oponopono & Law of Attraction Practitioner & a dōTERRA Wellness Advocate. She has also trained in EFT aka Tapping, Therapeutic Touch & Bio Energetic Awareness. Ordained as a Reverend from the Wisdom of the Heart Church, non-denominational spirituality & a reverence for Life are the foundations of her beliefs, along with the knowing that we are adored & provided for, by a Loving Source.

Kelly was with her partner of 15 years & the father of all her children, as he transitioned to the Other Side, due to a diagnosis of Pancreatic & Liver cancer. In a span of eight years, she experienced not only the loss of her partner but also the loss of her father, her only brother, her fifth child, her father, niece & grandmother in-law & four of the family's beloved dogs.

Grounded in her spiritual beliefs & Blessed by the Gifts of the Earth that would come into her Life, Kelly is able to 'keep on keeping on'& continues to thrive, living her Best Life Ever with joy & the knowingness that those on the Other Side are supporting her.

Kelly is working with people from many cultures & walks of Life experience the incredible power of natural solutions, bio-energetic awareness, & the ability to experience connection with Spirit. This gives way to finding a whole new & more empowering way to experience living our Best Lives Ever.

Website: www.Kellybaye.xyz

11

LEANNE WAKELING

2015 was the year of enlightenment. I began training to become a Professional Master Coach, which means learning the skills as well as enabling new thinking to evolve. Of course, at the beginning of 2015, I had no idea what the long-term effect was going to be.

The hindsight, the reality was, "I didn't know what I didn't know." I was the product of living as a human doing rather than living as a human being.

It's part of the challenge for many of us who grew up in a time where the needs of developing children were greatly misunderstood or unknown. Most adults today were brought up in a version of the authoritarian model of parenting. The "I'm the boss, I know better, do as you're told" model. Based in an assumption that children just need to be moulded into what was expected.

What I know now is there had been a societal gap in understanding the stages of the neurological development in a child. The assumption being that children arrive with all the hardware, and all we have to do is activate the software. In other words, all we had to do was program, that is teach them, what they needed to know as if they are an inexperienced version of an adult.

Neuroscience now informs us humans are born with only a 70-75% sized brain with 20% of its whole brain capability. Humans don't even have a whole brain until age ten (*The Whole Brain Child – Daniel Siegel and Tina Payne Bryson).* Even then, it's still got another 15ish years of development to go. What that means is that in the beginning, we do not have the skills, features, and capacity to do many of the things that have historically been the expectation.

There was the belief that children must be taught and therefore need to follow instructions. The patriarchal model of obedience became part of the tribal cycle. The problem is, this disregarded the nurture element that all humans NEED. Depending on the parent's own experience as to how skilled or not they were in being able to nurture. Providing a safe haven for a child to learn how to become themselves.

I'm still learning how to express healthy boundaries as part of my ongoing evolution on purpose. Boundaries being the gold standard method for enabling a child to learn how to BE.

Unfortunately, fear was far more likely to have been a tool in play, either using it to control or experiencing it and conceding to the child's apparent wishes. Certainly, many adults have poor relationships with one or more segments on the Circle of Security and their experience of the full range of emotions.

In our family, sadness seemed to be unwelcome. Only mum seemed to be allowed to experience sadness. This would tend to indicate that sadness was not part of the approved emotions when she was raised, so she reacted from her own discomfort. This is common across all of us with similar gaps. What a child needs is to have their emotions acknowledged, validated, and accepted so that the child can learn how to regulate that emotion.

It is never a child's responsibility to protect an adult's feelings. A difficult concept for some to embrace who were brought up to honour their elders. This does not mean that we don't support our child to learn, though is important not to judge them for their lack of experience.

Parenting is about the most important job in the world, yet it is the one that we have the least preparation for. Emotional literacy and human neurological development are examples of common parental knowledge gaps—these gaps impact when children start to develop the ability to express and manage various qualities intentionally.

The desire to "get things right" can catch some mothers in self-judgement. Wanting to be the best mum in the world and judging themselves when they slip and make mistakes along the way. Certainly, the experience I had, saw in my mum, and in lots of the mothers I serve now and have done over time.

The cognitive dissonance (*The state of having inconsistent thoughts, beliefs, or attitudes, especially as relating to behavioural decisions and attitude change)* is that even though we are adults, our parenting experience is only as old as our child.

Having been a child does not prepare us for parenting a child, particularly if we were not raised by emotionally mature parents that enabled us to gain the emotional resilience to BE a conscious and wholehearted adult. [1]

I have been seeking to evolve on purpose since my children were born. I wanted to be different to the way my mum had been without understanding what needed to happen in order to become different. The reality is that nature will always take the path of least resistance. What that means is that unless we've done work to change our programming, under stress, we default to the programming.

Change can be hard because we humans are wired for the familiar. It's part of our survival system to seek evidence of what it already knows to be true. That means we tend to be more suspicious of fresh ideas, and lots of us are more comfortable with "this is how we've always done it." I have to confess—this is my least favourite expression. Let us say, it's been my nemesis on more than one occasion, and it drives me to keep seeking new options and perspectives.

NO is only the first answer. I'm not generally easily defeated.

THE WORLD OF WORK

Given the above, you can imagine then how well I did in many of the environments I found myself in. I was what might be considered a rushing river in a world that prefers a quiet pond. On reflection, patience was not something that came easily, and social intelligence was a huge gap until the year of enlightenment.

I am the eldest of three girls, born into a military family at the time when society's attitudes were slowly shifting from where women were solely expected to be at home and raise a family.

It's been intriguing to have been privy to the evolution of attitudes and opportunities in society and, more particularly, with women in the workplace and the military throughout my lifetime.

The many evolutions that I have seen in the world of work are one of the reasons I find the subject of the future of work appealing. Workplaces and organisations are always needing to change and evolve to meet the needs of the changing landscape of the market.

Women and their relationship with their careers and lifestyle options began to be an interest to me when we were located in a somewhat regional area. As a military partner, I was frustrated with the attitudes to the military community and partners in particular as potential employees. Having been raised not to complain without having a solution I took the lead from a pilot program on returning to the workplace and commenced advocating for women and employment.

I also coordinated an annual seminar to explore the evolving diverse education options and employment pathways.

As the world of work evolves, it's been important to also encourage military partners and people, in general, to consider the word "career" in broader terms. Particularly with futurist forecasts that the workforce of 2050 looks more like the workforce from 1750 than 1950, our children need different skills to succeed.

That means that there'll be fewer opportunities for earning a living in the safety of a larger organisation and much more reliance on cottage industries and contracted service delivery that aligns to demand. We need to evolve with it and be involved in the design of its evolution.

While employment is something that contributes to life satisfaction, it is not the only means of creating life satisfaction.

MY SPIRITUAL JOURNEY

While more likely to be found exploring evidence and researched based material, my open mind means that I look at all things and explore them for what makes sense and how they fit into my belief system.   As someone who is incredibly curious, I explore lots of things from astrology to neuroscience to psychometric tools and assessments amongst many different ways of understanding humans and their behaviour.

I have a non-traditional relationship with my Christian faith. Probably because I was brought up in a military journey through the process. What that meant was never being indoctrinated into one arm of the faith. On bases, there were no more than two chapels, on for the Catholics and one for all the protestants. There was a roster of all the available protestant Chaplains to host Sunday services. Different bases could have different combinations of protestant representatives.   Eg   Methodists,   Presbyterian,   Anglican (Episcopalian), United, Baptist, Lutheran, Evangelical and sometimes even Salvation Army depending on the local team.   As a non-Catholic, this meant that we were served by whoever was the Chaplain on roster, meaning I was exposed to all the different protocols and beliefs. Leaving me open to all the various ways that faith may be expressed, even outside Christianity.

For me, the fundamental of the Christian faith is "being the hands of Jesus." For me, that means acceptance of people exactly where they are. To be non-judgemental. I am not an evangelist, and I do not usually share my faith. I am a believer in actions doing more than words.

The more I study, train, and research, the more layers I find that contribute to how we become individuals across the diversity of 8 billion people on the planet.

CROSS-GENERATIONAL FAMILY PSYCHOLOGY.

As I come on the journey of self-discovery and evolving on purpose, I become more and more fascinated at seeing the family system, the tribal cycle in action.

As I explored emotional intelligence as part of developing knowledge in Positive Psychology, I discovered I only had the foundations of the first pillar of emotional intelligence—Self-Awareness. I had much bigger gaps in the other pillars with barely the footings of Self-Management, Social Awareness, and Relationship Management.

As I recover the skills that were masked over to keep me safe, I am becoming more well-rounded, less volatile, more able to reciprocate and express healthy boundaries. I'm also noticing the ripple effect on the rest of the family system.

My journey has been learning how to be an emotional adult. This has been both confronting and freeing at the same time. I am learning to pause before responding and doing it without judgement, justification, or defensiveness.

It was what I began to appreciate about my mum and the way she reacted—watching the effects of her tribal cycle rippling onto us. She was shy and desperately wanted to be always doing the right thing.

Mum seemed to be quite emotionally unavailable for us girls—signs of her own anxiety and frustrations. Not that we appreciated that much at the time this contributed to resentments formed and held by an emotionally immature mind, mine!

It's only been in very recent times that I've begun to appreciate what my mother's experience in raising us must have been like for her.

As part of my journey building life coaching knowledge and expertise, I have added qualifications in DISC Behaviour and Meta DynamicsTM Thinking Styles profiling, certifications in Emotional Intimacy education, and Couples Counselling. I have also participated in parent education programs and mentored in the Positive Parenting arena online.

One of the things I love about all these different programs and tools has been learning and studying them has enabled me to gain skills in awareness and understanding of me. I particularly like DISC because it enables us to understand others and how they interpret their world as well, something that did not come so easily for me, as I was highly defensive until I began this self-discovery journey and began evolving on purpose.

The DISC model has a foundation of quadrants, Dominant, Influencer, Supporter and Compliance/Conscientious, hence the name of the tool. Each quadrant has some specific qualities, motivators and drivers that are different to the others. While we have all the qualities inside, the principle is about how easily or not we can access them. As a parent, and for relationships in general, this has been a key element empowering me to appreciate how others may view their world, instead of me thinking there was something wrong with me or take things personally.

As I reflected on mum's life through the lens of an extended DISC profiler*, I noticed some of the natural elements that contribute to her. I suspect her behaviour profile is the supporter. What I know of the supporter is that they don't like conflict, they need connection, and they don't like being in the spotlight or the centre of attention. They process their world slowly and need time to make decisions.

Her "shark music" (that soundtrack in our head from our childhood) often told her she was stupid because she took her time. The reality, she's quite intelligent but needs time to process. (An example of comparison being the enemy of joy.)

For her, her needs were the opposite of how she was being treated as a child and unsurprisingly why she became quite anxious.

I was the opposite when it came to behaviour style, which in itself created some conflict. I process my world fast, often speaking as or before I thought.

Both of us, due to our childhood experiences, developed hypervigilance due to factors that lead to disorganised attachment, which presented as reactivity.

Being so opposite meant I tended to receive lots of negative feedback from mum. Mum needed to feel in control and do things "the right way". My natural pace was somewhat overwhelming for her. Mostly because she didn't appreciate, nor could have had access to the knowledge that I just processed my world in a different way to her.

If only she had realised that she wasn't doing anything wrong. If only she'd understood that all I needed was her presence and to feel cared for. That is what all children need at the very foundations of the mother (primary carer)/child relationship.

MY PARENTING JOURNEY

When I became a parent, the only thing I really knew was that I didn't want to be like my mother. However, I had no real idea what that meant other than I didn't want my kids to feel the way I did—as in not good enough, always seeking approval, never feeling worthy, and being mad at me for not being their safe-haven.

In the beginning, I managed that intention really well. In fact, my husband has commented many times about how surprised he was on how well I did with our babies considering the minefield I could be at other times.

This zen changed as their personalities began to show up, and life became a lot more challenging. True to the tribal cycle, the shark music emerged. I'd be reactive and become really mad at myself, driving up the anxiety (that I didn't even know it was).

I did parenting programs to support me in managing the kids when they were young. It didn't stop them from being impacted by my behaviour as the programs were built on managing the children's behaviour, not my own. This was back in the late '80s and early '90s before much of the current knowledge around human neurological development was known.

I now appreciate the impact my reactivity had when my children were forming their own internal perspectives. I am learning to be compassionate with me, who was doing the best that I knew how and was capable of at the time.

I continue to learn that it is never too late to be healing both our inner child wounds or repairing and reclaiming the relationships we may have injured along the way.

As I continue evolving along my personal development journey, I gain more insight and clarity that as parents, the more we can focus on being a model of the type of person we want our child to become, the more likely we will raise children who will become the type of person we want them to be.

This is the real driver for the work I do supporting parents— particularly mothers who need to reclaim and heal their inner child so that they parent with confidence to become the type of person their children can model.

RAISING THE NEXT GENERATION

I get that it's tough for many adults these days when it comes to raising children. We are in the midst of the biggest transition in society and parenting in centuries. This change is driven by a combination of scientific progress in knowledge and understanding of human development and progress in the evolution in societal attitudes to practically everything, from how to have relationships to how the future of work will look.

The 21st century is shaping to be much more relationally focused. Hence children will need greater emotional intelligence in order to be resilient to the shifts.

Old world parenting worked on the fundamental that we had to form our children into the type of person who would be suitable for the big wide world of adulthood, in a time of a shift to mechanisation and need for conformance to the group.

New world parenting is about creating an environment that enables our children to become the best version of themselves. Building skills in emotional intelligence that enable creativity, necessary for adaptability, and the innovations that are the focus of the 21st century world of work.

Old world parenting was based on the premise that as long as the child conformed with instructions and expectations, they would be ok. This inevitably led to either or both parent and child to anxiety, frustration, and disappointment if a child was resistant.

The problem there becomes obvious. How can we possibly become a healthy, well-rounded, emotionally intelligent human who feels like they are enough, belong, and are loveable if most of the early years are filled with negative feedback about how we are being. It's how we progress to become human doings. The ideal is being able to evolve with ease along our development path, being guided by the provision of healthy boundaries. Instead, and without conscious intention from the way our parents act, we learn that there must be something wrong with us, and we need to behave in certain ways and evolve along the lines that we are told.

What we now know is not only that we don't have a whole brain until the age of ten, but that a brain is not at full capability until ages 24-28. The brain is not simply a muscle that needs to be strengthened through teaching from birth. It's an organ that evolves as our needs for support reduce. Our parenting evolves as our child develops.

We must appreciate that this level of knowledge has only been available since the early to mid 1990s with the evolution of knowledge in science that we've even been able to have the insight.

There will still be people who will find it difficult to take on the new information. It is only by evolving on purpose do we get to stay ahead of the curve.

For those of us who have been evolving and partner or co-parent with humans who find the evolution process difficult, we also need to be compassionate and considerate with those who process their world differently from us.

The reality is, in functional intimate relationships, we must be opposites. Not that we are not whole without the other party. It's that we are complimentary. Yin and Yang. Harmonious, not competitive.

To adults in relationships is to accept that other adults do not have to be like us in order for us to have a relationship with them. The key in adult-to-adult relationships is reciprocity. What that means is I can be like myself and express my boundaries. You can be like yourself and have your boundaries, and sometimes we'll bump stuff in the middle while we adjust to those boundaries.

I am now navigating through the repair process with my family. They are also on their own journey of healing from how I impacted their environment, with no conscious intention or awareness of the consequences.

What that meant was that instead of always being an emotionally intelligent safe haven for my children, I was always trying to manage how I was being. Do you relate?

This becomes exhausting.

MY PERSONAL EVOLUTION ON PURPOSE.

A key part of my awakening during my year of enlightenment in 2015 was that I had not been managing myself particularly successfully for some 50 odd years. Through finally busting that belief created as a little girl that "for me to be ok, I had to make sure EVERYONE was doing the right thing", I've now gone on to achieve so much more insight and learning. I am calmer, even more resilient, and feel better about myself.

It's a journey I now accept could never have been achieved alone. As the saying goes, you cannot solve a problem with the same thinking that created the problem. It's why I had spent so long on the merry-go-round of self-loathing. I am so grateful to the coaches who have served me along my way. The many awesome students at The Coaching Institute. Especially those of us who have been on the journey of reclaiming who we were meant to be before our tribal cycle took over.

The changes began in a moment, and once the doors were open, there was so much change available to me. The evolution is something my adult children comment on, as well as my sisters.

What I also notice is the change in my husband and my parents as well. This is particularly relevant to mum. As a product of her own upbringing, she was highly defensive, so sharing my journey has had to be approached delicately. This is not historically one of my strengths, but fortunately, amongst the skills, I am growing. I now have the social awareness that my journey was mine. Learning that it was ok to share, and healthy boundaries meant not judging others for whether they understood or agreed or not.

I've now taken hundreds of clients on the journey to fresh thinking, enabling them to improve their lives and relationships— fundamentally changing the relationship they have with themselves.

What I love most is the change in the environment that their children are forming their identity in—enabling my mission through empowering the parents.

THE CHALLENGE

The challenge for some of us on a journey of intentional change can be becoming a zealot in the process. We reinforce our own need for proof by ensuring that others agree with us. OR we intentionally or unintentionally judge those who have not come on the journey as somehow inferior. In either case, we commit a boundary violation when we cross that line into judgement.

We humans can get so bent out of shape trying to justify or defend ourselves over things that in the big scheme of living are not that important. Our body responds, based on the meanings we created usually long before the situation we are reacting/responding to. When the trigger is to verbal feedback, if we agree, it's accepting, even if we don't like it, we have information to prompt change. Instead of getting mad, we can be grateful for the insight.

Our beliefs and attitudes affect how we create, build and sustain relationships. When our foundations are flawed, we are destined to repeat our tribal cycle without conscious intention.

MY MISSION

To enable 1 million children to become emotionally intelligent and resilient adults so that they can navigate the 21st century with the tools, strategies, and skills to succeed.

My pathway to this is educating, enabling, and empowering their primary carers/parents/mothers to discover their own inner worth and self-trust so that they are models of excellence of how to BE in the world, which means that the family journey together with less friction, more harmony and enables the adults to parent with confidence and be the leaders with their family.

The mission isn't to change who we are, it is to rediscover, reclaim and restore the qualities that may have been lost or hidden along the way—keeping the qualities and beliefs that serve us well and update the ones that no longer serve.

We are not rejecting who we are, rather we are choosing to find the person we were meant to be before the input from the tribe was imposed.

In the process, we become the model of who we want our children to become, the qualities we want them to embrace. Easing the pathway of the Disciple, who is learning from who we are way before they ever learn from what we say.

We get to reclaim and heal the inner child, empowering us to become our Ultimate Self, enabling us to be a Conscious Wholehearted Adult, Parent with Confidence, and create harmony at home.

https://www.facebook.com/LeanneGWakeling
https://www.facebook.com/groups/raisingwholeheartedadults
https://www.linkedin.com/in/leannewakeling/
https://leannegwakeling.com.au

1. *Conscious chosen from The Conscious Parent by Dr. Shefali Tsabary and Wholehearted from the work of Brene Brown.*
    https://brenebrown.com/wholehearted-inventory/

ABOUT THE AUTHOR
LEANNE WAKELING

Leanne is a relationship coach, parenting mentor, behaviour and thinking styles profiler. She's had a diverse career across the military, public and private sector in administration and logistics before entering the coaching world in 2015.

She has four now adult children and her passion is empowering mothers to know they are enough through experiencing life satisfaction so that they have the emotional capacity to raise their family to thrive emotionally and socially through the rollercoaster of the challenges of the 21st century.

Leanne's passion comes from her lifelong work advocating for acceptance of both herself, and championing those that she comes into contact with. It is only in recent years that she became empowered to know that she is enough, just as she is.

Like many, she was brought up by parents who were doing the best they knew how and were capable of.

For many years she blamed her parents for the lack of acceptance she had in herself. The contradiction of the inner rebel fighting to fit and the fear of rejection. Leading to volatility that originated with the belief of not being enough formed in the mind of a young child.

This has led to her mission to enable 1 million children to be raised to become emotionally intelligent and resilient adults through educating enabling and empowering their parents to have healthy relationships and become their ultimate selves with self-trust and self-love so that their children are raised with models of excellence in emotional maturity.

Leanne is a lifelong learner who believes we are either green and growing, or ripe and rotting so generously shares her knowledge, experience and wisdom as she navigates her own evolution on purpose.

Page: www.facebook.com/LeanneGWakeling
Profile: www.facebook.com/leanne.wakeling.2/
Group: www.facebook.com/groups/raisingwholeheartedadults

12

LIBBA PHILLIPS ©
LISTENING TO HEAVEN

*C*ould the worst thing that ever happened to you ultimately lead you to your life purpose? I would have never imagined that would be my conclusion during the darkest days of my life.

Grateful to be home after a long day at work, I almost ignored the insistent ringing of my phone. Before I could even say hello, I heard my younger sister's frantic voice on the line, "Ashley is missing! We got a tip that she was seen a few days ago wandering on Dale Mabry near downtown Tampa. Our parents have been to the police, but they won't file a missing person's report!"

"What do you mean?!" I demanded. "Our insurance company dropped us. The treatment center released her without telling anyone. She left all her things and walked out the front door." I felt the room spinning, my heart began racing, and panic set in.

In a mental frenzy, I booked the next flight home. I hurriedly called the vet to see if they could board the cats for a week and called my boss before I could rehearse what to say. In a state of shock, I'm sure I wasn't making much sense trying to explain something I didn't even understand. I don't remember driving to the airport, but I got on the next plane home—determined to find my sister myself.

The early days of searching were a blur. My family and I tacked up homemade flyers, like the faded ones you see with a reward for a lost dog's return, on telephone poles and in storefront windows. We made desperate daily phone calls and stopped at hospitals, jails, and homeless shelters, but were often stonewalled and turned away. "Maybe your sister doesn't want to be found," we were told, and "we have to respect privacy laws." Hearing this over and over, I flew into a rage. I found myself screaming.... "I don't give a shit about your privacy laws! I need to know where my sister is right now!" "Miss, if you don't leave, I'll call the police and report you for harassment." It just didn't seem to matter to anyone in authority that she was lost, out of her mind, and extremely vulnerable. I remember being callously told by one police officer, "if she gets caught using drugs, THEN it's our problem." He may as well have slapped me in the face as he dismissed my repeated plea to file a missing person's report.

I stormed back to my rental car in the precinct parking lot. Sickened with anger and pounding my hands on the steering wheel, I entertained thoughts of storming back into the police station and making a scene with my demands. But I knew that snapping back would not find my sister.

Now on our own, my family and I soon changed tactics and began to approach homeless people on street corners. We quickly realized that giving out rolled-up dollar bills and packs of cigarettes to transient strangers got people to look at Ashley's flyer and talk to us. Some sent us on wild goose chases down dead-end roads, and others shared their own horrible stories that filled me with dread about the realities of being on the streets. At 8 am each morning, I called the morgue to inquire about any unidentified deceased Jane Does, instead of lounging over a second cup of coffee and my weekly sales reports. I was shocked to learn that there were over 40,000 unidentified deceased persons in the United States. Why did no one know who they were? They belonged to someone, didn't they?

We scouted known drug areas after dark each night, which brought me face to face with the evil reality of prostitution and sex trafficking. Menacing looking thugs went on the defense as we approached defeated looking girls in short shorts and skimpy tops on street corners. I remember one girl got in my face and said, "Get the hell outta here. You're not safe," as she fearfully looked towards several men standing in front of a liquor store keeping guard of their assets. Shaking, but determined they would not see me cry, I got back into the car. The days turned to weeks with no sign of my sister, and eventually, I had to return to my life and my job in California without answers.

I was consumed with worry with each passing day and continually haunted by a premonition I'd had a few months earlier. As I hugged my sister goodbye after a holiday visit at Christmas—I was struck with a foreboding sense in the pit of my stomach that I would never see her again. I relived that moment over and over in my mind. Was there something I could have done to have prevented this?

After all the weeks of searching, I began to realize that if Ashley was not listed as missing, the odds of her ever being found, if she was still alive, were slim. And how would she be identified if she was dead somewhere? She had no form of identification or driver's license with her on the day she disappeared and walked into the abyss. I was tormented by the vision that she was lying dead somewhere, decomposing into skeletal remains.

I continued my daily calls to every morgue and medical examiner across the state of Florida, hoping that someone, somewhere, would help us. One empathetic coroner suggested that we try to obtain any dental records for 'just in case' Ashley turned up as a deceased Jane Doe in the state. Again—I argued—that without that missing person report being filed—who is going to make the connection that a Jane Doe could be Ashley to match the dental records to? With tears streaming down my face, I hung up the phone, feeling completely defeated.

I didn't think the nightmare could get any worse, but I was proven wrong by yet another telephone call that brought me to my knees. "Your Grandfather is dying," my mother said. "He has just a few days to live. You need to come back home now to say goodbye." I choked back sobs as I packed once more for another cross-country trip to see him one last time.

My grandparents were the only example of kindness and stability I had as a child. My Grandaddy Bob was a minister who wore his heart on his sleeve. He often prayed with his parishioners and complete strangers at the grocery store as if their troubles were his own. And while I secretly hoped his words of faith were true, I carried a deep sense of abandonment about my estranged father and anger about the abusive adopted one that took his place. I often wondered where was this invisible God my grandfather had devoted his life to?

Sitting at his deathbed, I quietly raged to the silent unseen. "My sister is missing, my job is on the line, and letting your biggest fan die from colon cancer is just wrong. Feel free God to jump in anytime." But even in his final hours, my Granddaddy wanted to pray with me and assure me about what was next. I was thinking to myself his God would never hear those prayers. I didn't believe He existed.

I will always remember our final exchange. Grandaddy Bob reached out to take both of my hands. He said, "Libba, God answers prayers —sometimes the answer doesn't come right away, but it comes. But you must get quiet. Listen."

"How can he have faith even as he suffers like this?" I thought to myself, with tears rolling down my cheeks, as I held his frail hands for the last time. Even as his life force was slipping away, there was conviction in his voice as he spoke his final words to me, "Libba, everyone has a purpose, including you—and when I get there—as he pointed to the sky—I'm going to see about that."

He died the next day. And in the days that passed, it became clear to me through a series of coincidences, unexplainable dreams that showed glimpses of my future, and a chance meeting with someone who suggested I start a nonprofit organization, that I was being divinely guided to be the answer to my own prayer. I felt a quiet but strong knowing that I needed to 'do something'— not only for myself but also for other families looking for missing loved ones lost among the homeless.

I grabbed an old notebook and began writing down ideas and thoughts that came to me. They seemed to pour into my mind like a classroom of noisy children, all clamoring to be heard. At first, I wondered if maybe I was going crazy. After all, I was a classic 'Type A' personality with a job as a pharmaceutical sales rep whose focus was meeting sales quotas and getting my expense reports in on time. Communicating with angels in my living room and receiving what I now know to be 'divine downloads' did not fit the narrative I had for my life! That would all change after I got my first major media interview about my sister's disappearance after dozens of rejections by the local news stations. I had the unshakeable feeling my Grandaddy was making good on his promise.

But I didn't know I would see the evidence revealed in a doctor's exam room! "What brings you in today?" my OB/GYN asked with a smile. "Well, certainly not my desire to wear this paper gown made for people half my size!" I replied. "Had any major life changes since I last saw you? Lie down on the table and tell me what's news. It will help make this go by quicker."

My stomach clenched as I took a deep breath, and the examination began. "Well—my sister disappeared several months ago. The police won't file a missing person's report, and I can't get anyone to listen to me. I really need someone big to help me tell my story. Someone like Jennifer Smith at News 10—then people might listen!"

The doctor looked up, with tears in her eyes, bringing her gaze directly to mine. "Libba, you won't believe this—but Jennifer Smith is a good friend. I can't promise anything but let me give her a call and see what I can do." I felt a tingle down my spine and goosebumps on my arms—but it wasn't from being barely clothed in the doctor's office! Surely 'this' was not just a coincidence.

Leaving the parking lot, I was still mulling over the connection and wondering what it would be like to meet Jennifer Smith. In my mind, I could see her in her trademark red suit, and I started mentally rehearsing what I would say if she actually called me. I literally gasped and shouted, "Oh My God!" to no one as the giant city bus roared past me to change lanes on the freeway. The entire side of the bus was wrapped with the super-sized smiling face of Jennifer Smith and the News 10 logo! I had to pull over to catch my breath and sobbed all the way home feeling a sense of wonder and hope.

It was only a couple of hours later that I got a telephone call from Jennifer Smith herself. "I would really like to interview you and make you my next feature story to air this weekend. Are you available tomorrow afternoon at 5 o'clock?" When the doorbell rang the next day, I was stunned to see Jennifer standing in my front doorway, with her cameraman and his Sony professional camcorder on his shoulder, extending her hand to shake mine. I knew, without any doubt, that a force greater than myself, was helping me. I held fast to that belief in the days and years to come.

I called the nonprofit organization Outpost for Hope. It started as a website for me to log my information and to assist others who faced the same roadblocks. It quickly became apparent that I was not the only one frustrated by what I call the 'the revolving door'. Most of our nation's homeless with mental illness and/or addiction revolve through the doors of emergency rooms, jails, the streets, sometimes reconnecting with family members, and then usually end up back out onto the streets without a safety net over and over. I knew that what I was seeing was a bigger problem. The 'missing, missing', as I called this population, were also easy targets for abuse and exploitation. I knew that not all homeless people were lost, but my experience revealed to me that there were many who were. My sister was one of them.

Some success stories happened—and loved ones were reconnected with their families. But I quickly had to re-define what a success story is, as many searching families can attest that sometimes 'finding someone' is not always a happy ending. It is almost impossible to bring someone home from being lost on the streets, who has possibly been traumatized and/or exploited, and expect him or her to be stable without the right care and support.

Eventually, I left my corporate job as a pharmaceutical sales rep to run the nonprofit effort full time. And while I knew that I was being divinely guided, this journey was certainly no walk in the park with angels leaving rose petals to soften my steps. I continued going into dangerous dark alleys, drug houses, and morgues looking for my sister and carried the weight of despair from many other families who were also searching for lost loved ones. I knew that I had to find some relief, or I may not survive the reality for long. On a whim, I walked into a bookstore that advertised a class on meditation. "I may as well see if this works because I can't sleep at night, and I need a break." Fidgeting in my seat and mentally rehearsing my 'to do' list reminded me that I would most likely not become a yogi anytime soon. But I loved the hypnotic sound of the teacher's voice and the faint smell of incense in the cozy room in the back of the bookstore. It gave me a sense of reassurance that I could choose peace instead of anxiety—at least for thirty minutes. I was often surprised to find that I had been 'away' when the teacher guided us to 'come back' afterwards.

After a few weeks of practicing meditation, I found that my thoughts were slightly more organized and my intuition clearer. I became obsessed with learning everything I could about the power of the mind, angels, and the law of attraction. Books by Sophy Burnham,

Joseph Campbell, and Wayne Dyer piled up on the floor by my bedside. Each morning when I woke up, I would read a little and journal my requests to the divine for help. At night I would review what 'breadcrumbs' or 'coincidences', or 'answers' would come. I was often stunned at the outcomes. I started keeping track of those experiences, like the time I was given a cancerous tumor diagnosis and the guidance I received about how to get better. And how I made a connection with the attending nurse in the recovery room after my surgery who 'just happened' to have a missing sister too. There are too many of those coincidences and stories to list here. But I was constantly reminded that I was not alone. It was usually me, and my own despairing thoughts, that would block that guidance on more difficult days. But when I did listen, I acted upon that guidance, and a 'next step', or 'amazing connection' was often revealed.

Several years into the search for my sister, my family still didn't have success getting the missing person's report filed. It would ultimately take the persistent efforts of my best friend who continually advocated on our behalf, to finally get law enforcement to file a report; four years after the fact. By this time, my sister's trail had long grown cold, along with any meaningful investigation that could have made a difference. But having that report was at least an acknowledgement that she was, in fact, missing.

At this point, I had a front-row seat to the dark reality and a growing sense of injustice that this problem of 'missing, missing' persons was bigger than just my sister and needed to be heard by a larger audience. What else could I do? I had success finally, thanks to Jennifer Smith, in being in the local news, but what about the national media? I quickly wrote out an ideal scene that I was hoping for in my notebook, asked my angels for help, and waited. For a while, nothing seemed to be happening. But I continued to receive the message to be patient and trust in divine timing. For fun, I gathered some colored markers, a bottle of glue, and a pair of scissors and created a collage of that ideal scene on a piece of yellow construction paper. I cut out the logo of People magazine that was sitting on my coffee table, typed up a pretend story about the mission and the journey to find my sister, and put it inside a folder for safekeeping. I stayed quiet about my request but knew that if this was something that 'should' happen, it would. Learning to trust in divine timing was a lesson I would learn repeatedly.

I didn't know whether to laugh or cry when almost a year later to the day I had made my request to the heavens for my story to be seen in front of a larger audience, when a friend with media connections called me and asked, "Do you want to be interviewed by People magazine for a feature article?" That would be the beginning of many more articles, news stories, and speaking engagements to come.

Several close friends witnessed what was happening in my life and asked me how I was doing it. I began to quietly teach what I was learning to small groups in my home and began to see transformations occurring in other people's lives too. I also kept journaling about what I was experiencing and the realizations that were unfolding for me.

My grandfather was right—God does answer prayers. But sometimes the answer is "Not yet. Wait. Or I have a bigger plan in mind." I realized that our loved ones in heaven, including angels and beloved grandparents, for example, can and do communicate with us. We just have to know how to interpret the signs and stay in faith even when nothing seems to be happening. It is wonderfully reassuring to know that life does indeed 'go on', and we have a team of helpers who walk with us. It's just up to us to learn how to receive the guidance that we are given and to take inspired action. And though I wasn't initially receptive to the idea that 'God' existed, He showed up. While he didn't magically appear to me like the wise Gandalf in Harry Potter, he revealed his steady, consistent presence through the very real outcomes that occurred.

I've put into practice the concepts of 'manifesting' and 'Law of Attraction' now for the last 20 plus years. And I've observed people become disillusioned with it seemingly 'not working'. But maybe the reason why the 'situation' or whatever someone has been visualizing appearing on their doorstep isn't coming, for example, is because they haven't taken steps to go for that new job or write that book or put in the actual work that's needed for it to happen. Perhaps there are blocks to having 'it', or some other reason that having 'it' is not currently part of 'what's next'. But if you can stay un-attached to the outcome, I promise you that the universe can come up with something remarkable that is in alignment with your desires. Prayers and intentions are how we make our requests known, but the answers might show up as a 'chance meeting' or a call from 'out of the blue' or some other intuitive nudge that guides you to the next step. I've learned that sometimes the 'challenge' we are having is really an opportunity in disguise that reveals a bigger purpose or plan. I began my journey with one goal, to find my sister and bring her safely home. And while I didn't get the happy ending that I had hoped for, God walked with me through a very difficult journey that was used for a larger purpose to help many other families with lost loved ones while raising awareness about these issues around the world.

I became pregnant at age 41 and heard the familiar divine whisper that it was time for a new chapter in my life. Once again, I reached out to the heavens for help. I wanted to focus on preparing for motherhood and step back from advocacy work. I still hoped that awareness about 'missing, missing' persons would grow so that perhaps someday perception and policy changes would occur and no one else would ever have to endure what my family did. For a few years, my best friend and I had gathered information and recorded interviews with coroners, police, and forensic specialists. We'd hoped to make a documentary film but ultimately put the project down until we could raise the funds or the right help to put it all together. That desire for awareness was ever present in my mind when I made the request to the heavens that a 'way' would be shown or given if it was still a priority to God. I stuck that request on a magnet on my refrigerator and trusted 'that, or something better' was done. A few days later, I got a call 'out of the blue' asking if I would be interested in the story of the search for my sister becoming a Lifetime television movie. It wasn't the documentary project I had planned for, but it was God's way, of taking the reins and raising awareness about the 'missing, missing' in a way I never could. 'Bringing Ashley Home' premiered in the US in 2011 and has been seen in over 20 countries around the world.

After more than two decades of trying to follow Ashley through the revolving door, her exact location is unknown to me today. And for now, I must surrender her life and her whereabouts to God. I realize that it may sound cliché - but during the darkest nights of my soul, searching for my sister, I found a resolve within me that I didn't know existed. I learned to trust my intuition when I had absolutely nothing else or no one else, to rely on.   I learned that prayers are answered, but I need to listen to what the answer actually is. Because of those prayers and intentions, I was guided to the next step on the journey and to opportunities that made a difference for many other people and myself. God has revealed to me that we all have a direct connection to the divine to help bring solutions to problems, to bring our dreams to life, and to live with faith no matter what difficulties we face.   He told me then that someday I would be teaching these concepts to others and that's what I do now!

The state of our world today needs your unique light if humanity is to evolve and bring more peace to our planet. You have that special 'something' that no one else has.   What gives you joy?   What causes are you passionate about?   What difficulties have you personally overcome or are dealing with right now? What do you feel a sense of urgency about accomplishing? Your answers to these questions are a good place to start discovering what your life purpose is.

I've heard it said that purpose is simply that thing you want your life to be about more than any other. It's that dream that won't leave you alone or that desire to make a difference using the gifts and talents you already possess to bring it to reality. All your life experiences up until now, especially your greatest challenges and deepest heartaches, have helped to specifically prepare you to do so. Your 'mess' may very well be 'your message'. You are a spark of the Divine, and every part of you is designed to express that!

Are you tired of feeling lost and disoriented? Ready to turn setbacks into triumphs? Want to create miracles even better than you can imagine? Let this be your divine sign that you no longer need to go it alone. Visit the Intuitive Navigator to tap into the miraculous guidance of Heaven. www.theintuitivenavigator.com

ABOUT THE AUTHOR
LIBBA PHILLIPS

Libba is an Intuitive Guide, Miracle Mindset Coach and the creator of The Divine Messenger Method™. She helps people around the world connect to divine guidance - so they can triumph over difficult setbacks and manifest what is in their highest good.

After Libba's sister disappeared over 20 years ago, she began receiving messages from God, her beloved grandparents, and the angels. As a result of that guidance, she created Outpost for Hope, a social justice movement to shine the light on at-risk children and adults who are often lost among the homeless. At the beginning of that journey, there was no media or law enforcement support to help find her sister or to raise awareness about the 'missing, missing' population. But as Libba acted on the guidance she received, she began to be featured in major publications including Reader's Digest & People Magazine and eventually went on to inspire a Lifetime television movie. Libba never spoke publicly until now about the heavenly help behind the scenes that made it all happen.

Today it is Libba's purpose to share the message that we are all divinely guided, we just need to pay attention to the guidance we receive from the heavenly realms. Libba says we all have access to the navigational tools that will awaken us to our divine life purpose and help us create a more fulfilling life. She helps clients transform their own lives through her mentoring sessions, online courses, and workshops. If you want to co-create a life that is even better than you can imagine, learn more at www.theintuitivenavigator.com

Facebook:
www.facebook.com/theintuitivenavigator
Instagram:
www.instagram.com/libbatheintuitivenavigator/

13

LIDIA KULESHNYK

HOW TO HEAL AND BECOME THE CONSCIOUS LEADER OF YOUR LIFE

CENTERED. CONNECTED. CONSCIOUS™

"*When The Leaves Fall Wet, Off The Darkened Branches. When Gold And Crimson Lay Their First Blanket. When The Wind Does Share Its Haunting Breath. . . That Is When. . . I'll Call . . .To Death*"

I wrote this poem after my second near-death experience. It changed my life forever.

EVOLVING

Death and rebirth . . . the necessary, and sometimes painful, initiations in the journey of life.

They are part of evolution. . .the process of healing and transformation that takes you to a higher place of being, of inner ease and knowing. . . the place of security within you where you no longer feel the pull of doubt, guilt, shame, or fear. . . the state of being that feels so solid in your gut that you know you can handle any situation that may arise. As you evolve on purpose, you realize you are eternal and safe in the arms of the universe . . . you return to wholeness, conscious of the oneness . . .committed to your self-mastery, accepting responsibility for yourself. . and knowing. . . all will be well.

To continuously evolve and experience higher and easier states of being is what I came here to do. As my macrobiotic teacher, Michio Kushi, taught, we are evolving from "homo sapiens to homo spiritus," from an intellectually-based operating system to a spiritually-based operating system. This transformation is happening now.

The time of great change is upon us. This "shift of the ages" has been prophesized for eons of time, dating back to ancient civilizations 18,000 years ago. As a collective, we're in for quite a ride as we surf the waves of upheaval and uncertainty. .. the change leading us into the paradigm of light. We are rapidly moving to 2100 when the north pole aligns with the north star, heralding in the next 13,000 years of light.

This paradigm of light is being consciously created now. The future is being created by you. What world are you creating through your thoughts, choices, desires, and actions? What legacy do you want to leave? What imprint will you create for others to embrace? And how do you create this?

CREATING PARADISE

As a mindful ancestor. .. as a conscious, humane steward of this planet . . . how do you create the foundation for future generations? How do you create a pathway that honours life, the integrity of your soul, and the soul of the planet? You create this by healing yourself. At this time in history, healing yourself is the greatest accomplishment you will ever achieve. For in doing so, you are creating a foundation from which you can develop a deep relationship with yourself, the inner knowing that you have the inherent strength to live in both the material and spiritual worlds. . . you are a conscious bridge for this union. At this time in history, you are also bridging the old dark paradigm and the emerging paradigm of light. And to be here on Earth right now, to live in both worlds, is a sign of your inherent self-mastery. "Know Thyself and Thou Shalt Know The Universe" the ancient tablets state.

As you heal, you transform and grow. .. you expand your capacity to be more, do more, live more . . . you evolve. You begin to connect with your essence, your worth, and your value. You begin to remember who you are. You honour yourself as a powerful spiritual being, humble and great in your presence, a conscious leader, first of yourself, then for others. You are able to shift your focus from "where you are" to "who you are" and begin to live a life that is grounded, energized, and focused, a life of lasting self-empowerment. You create a foundation of being centered-connected-conscious™ and are able to understand why you came here and what is your purpose and mission. As I like to say, *We didn't come here to live in paradise. We came here to create paradise.* Through your healing and return to wholeness, you evolve on purpose and live as the mindful ancestor of future generations.

THE JOURNEY OF DEEP HEALING: TURNING LEAD INTO GOLD

My journey of healing began at the age of 10. I decided I no longer wanted to live with chronic pain and be dependent on others for support. I was born with deformed organs that created secondary health problems, including digestive and endocrine disorders. Because my condition was difficult to label and diagnose, the medical community was limited in how they could help. I remember being told my kidneys were weak, and my spleen essentially didn't function at all. I remember asking doctors why my body could not digest food.

I was eventually viewed as a psychosomatic patient by doctors who thought my symptoms were imaginary. But I never gave up.

I always knew that there must be someone out there who could help me! *Not Recovering Is Not An Option* was the mantra I created and posted on my sinks, light switches, and mirrors. I visualized the life that I wanted . . . a life free of physical pain . . . and I imagined myself living it as if I had already achieved it. I wanted a simple life of health, happiness, and peace, living in a cabin, eating whole foods, surrounded with the love and power of wild animals. I wanted to be Caroline Ingalls from Little House On The Prairie! I made a fort in our ravine to start to live that which I desired . . . making mud pies, sitting in a circle of stones in a poplar grove with the butterflies, fox, and raven by my side. I began to heal myself in the way that felt right, regardless of the differing voices of the world.

I remember walking down the grassy driveway by my barn, on a hot, humid August day, at the age of 12, declaring to the universe, "I want to be whole and free." I yearned to experience the depth of the elemental world . . . the intoxicating smells of the soil, blossoms, trees. . the ethereal union with the wind, moon, stars. ..the raw chill of the rain, snow, and sleet against my cheek. I knew I could be free of the burden of physical weakness. I just wanted to be an average healthy person. I didn't know that my journey to create physical health would take me into the greatest depths of my soul.

I have passed through the doorway, into your soul. That torturous journey has made me whole, I wrote one day. I didn't realize it at the time, but because I had to change the actual structure of my being, my cells, tissues, organs, in order to achieve "basic health", I had to experience transformation at the deepest level. I never felt defeated emotionally or mentally. My soul called me to liberate myself out of my earthly struggle. Every day was an exhausting exercise to merely survive. I had to heal my weakest link, my physical body. I knew that once I healed my weakest link, my life would become easy . . . from the inside out. I began to realize *You Are Only As Strong As Your Weakest Link.*

When I started this journey to reclaim my health and regain my energy, I never imagined the expansive world of light and unconditional love that I would initiate myself into right here on Earth. I declared to myself *I didn't come to this planet to be half-alive.* My true journey was beyond creating physical well-being . . . my journey was to refine my power.

THE JOURNEY OF DEEP HEALING: CONSCIOUS LEADERSHIP

At the age of 27, I was guided by dreams to eat macrobiotically and visit Michio Kushi, the forefather of macrobiotics. It was through my dreams, my spiritual connection, that I found the solution to my problem. "For Every Problem, There Is A Solution," my teacher often shared. It was Michio Kushi who explained to me the complexity of the conditions with which I was born. He also recognized the hard work I had been doing for 17 years to try to heal myself. But Michio explained that if I continued on the path I was on, "You will never know true health in your lifetime" because the improvement in my health was slow and difficult. Hearing him say those words startled me. I asked myself *how all of my hard work could not create the life I so desperately wanted?* The methods I had been using were helpful but not powerful enough to heal me at the deepest level. I followed Michio Kushi's macrobiotic dietary recommendations, having no interest at the time, to understand them. I just did it. I followed the recipes, cooked and chewed the food. And I began to transform from the inside out. I could feel something shift deep within. It was magnificent!

As a child, when I was in pain, I used my mind to separate myself from my physical body. Without realizing it, I had mastered separation of mind and body, not through denial and repression, not through detachment, but through non-attachment. This is how I learned the principles of Taoist non-attachment. I lived them. Then later, I learned about what I had lived and the labels given to them. *When you live something, you know it to be true,* I soon understood. As I experienced the power of my own healing, I had no doubt about the effectiveness of the methods that came to me in dreams. Macrobiotics and reiki had healed my constitution, the body I was born with, which is a truly incredible accomplishment. I reclaimed my health, regained my energy, and refined my power. I became the conscious leader of my life.

IN SERVICE TO THE ONENESS: NON-ATTACHMENT AND THE CAPACITY PRINCIPLE

My most memorable prophetic dreams were in my cocoon of healing . . . dreams about the coming of the great light . . . dreams in which I died and was reborn. I was shown symbols on the horizon and layers of the earth changing in frequency. I was shown the state of organs in my body and how to heal. I saw myself carrying frying pans full of water up steep cliffs . . . and white light coming out of my hands. Beautiful white beings spoke to me in dreams. Some turned into ravens, some turned into horses . . . some just had a good belly laugh with me. But one thing they always were . . . was persistent.

When I started to reclaim my health, I thought I would go back to my career as an environmental policy analyst. It took many dreams, with very clear messages, to convince me to leave that profession and start offering reiki, macrobiotic and holistic counselling services. In addition to my degrees in zoology, environmental science, and animal behavior, I had a bachelor of science degree in psychology, so counselling made sense to me at the time. But when I had dreams of people lining up at my door, waiting for reiki and macrobiotic healing, I was a bit uncertain about this whole "spiritual guidance" thing. My experience had proven that certain types of dreams were messages of specific action, but those had been for my own healing. Now I was being guided . . . more like inundated . . . with messages to start my professional healing practice! I just couldn't ignore the power of these messages.

I started seeing clients through referrals. One year turned into three . . . and the dreams I had years before, of line-ups at my door, turned into reality. I decided to let go of any opportunities that came my way for the perfect policy job and "went with the flow"! And what a flow of energy and abundance it has been . . . 25 years in professional practice helping clients heal their chronic health conditions. .. and 22 years running my own horse rescue sanctuary! Interestingly, I never had an intention or desire to do either. Through my own healing, I simply became a powerful channeler of information and energy . . . with a clarity that is as real as the material world but far greater than the intellect can surmise. It was through my dreams that I received the communications and soul unions reminding me of who I truly was . . . what my soul missions were. . . and how easily it all unfolds when you align yourself with your essence through your commitment to healing.

I offered the approaches that I knew healed my "incurable" health conditions. I had full confidence in my ability to support others who also had difficult, chronic health conditions. I have been honoured to support clients in their unique healing journeys, to help them remember who they are, and become the conscious leaders of their lives. After two decades of offering reiki, macrobiotics, and holistic coaching separately, I found that the most efficient and effective approach is to combine all three modalities so clients can achieve the greatest results in the shortest amount of time. I call this approach my Apona Healing Method. As a Chronic Health Specialist and Health and Energy Coach, I utilize 12 ancient principles as part of my Apona Healing Method. The first principle is "Everything is Energy" (which I have most certainly lived!), and the 12th principle is my "Capacity Principle of Conscious Leadership and Success: Know Your Limit, Live Within It."

If you really want to heal and release the toxins, the old beliefs, imprints, and trauma, at their deepest root, then reiki and macrobiotics can take you as deep as you want to go. And with your own self-reflection or with the support of a coach, you can connect the process of healing with your self-empowerment, in your own time and in your own way. You can learn these tools yourself or seek guided support. You are never alone. I am here to support you. If I had to choose one tool to empower you for life, a tool that you could use anytime, anywhere, it would be my Capacity Principle.

The Capacity Principle is based on Taoist non-attachment principles and learning how to recognize your energetic state of being so that you do not use more energy throughout the day than your present capacity. This is part of the art of living, knowing when to apply oneself and when to pull back, so that your core energy always remains strong enough to meet its major demands of (1) basic biological functioning (2) mental-emotional requirements (3) demands of external stressors and (4) providing substantial and powerful energy to heal a chronic health condition. Through strengthening your core energy, you expand the energetic capacity of your cells, supporting healing and personal growth. By learning The Capacity Principle, burnout, exhaustion, depletion, and chronic fatigue are avoided, and you can continue to balance your life with enough energy and vitality to face any circumstance with inner ease. You develop a confidence beyond intellect, the confidence of knowing that you are the "captain of your ship" and you can face the future with the security of your own state of being . . . your refined power.

The Capacity Principle is the 12th Principle and culmination of 11 Ancient Principles in my Apona Healing Method.

1. Everything Is Energy
2. Energy Never Lies, You Can't Fool Mother Nature.
3. For Every Problem, There Is A Solution.
4. Everything That Happens To You Is What You Lack. All That Is Antagonistic, Unbearable Is Complementary.

5. Everything That Has A Front Has A Back. The Bigger The Front. The Bigger The Back.
6. Everything That Has A Beginning Has An End.
7. Everything Changes (aka Change is the Constant of The Universe).
8. There Is Nothing Identical.
9. Divine Alignment, Is Divine Timing (aka There Is No Insignificant Action).
10. You Are Only As Strong As Your Weakest Link.
11. Yin and Yang Are Greater Than Willpower.
12. The Capacity Principle: Know Your Limit, Live Within It.

By moving through your healing journey with the awareness of at least one of these principles, you can more easily live in the state of Taoist non-attachment. . . full presence, commitment, and engagement in life without absorbing external influences. You become the Buddha sitting in the middle of the burning inferno. . . untouched by the events around you.

THE TIME IS NOW

The time is now for you to shine and ground the light, to create and share great abundance for all. Abundance is the essence of the universe. The old principles of the last 13,000 years, isolation and separation, are out of order with the universe. They are being released. Connection and unity, true principles of the universe, of the oneness of life, are being activated for awakening and growth. The light of 2100 is on its way!

Whatever problem or challenge you are dealing with, the solution already exists. Don't give up when your soul calls. When the soul is urging you to move forward, but your mind and emotions are not yet ready to act, the resistance builds up in your body as stress, tension, anxiety, overwhelm, depression, or physical ailments. Take action to activate your core energy, to release the energy stuck in your body.

The flow of your energy is critical to keeping your life force strong so that you can heal and evolve.

Health, happiness, and peace are your birthright. Reclaim them. Live a centered-connected-conscious life and feel the joy and fulfillment of becoming the mindful ancestor for future generations.

ABOUT THE AUTHOR
LIDIA KULESHNYK

Lidia Kuleshnyk, B.Sc., M.E.S., is a Chronic Health Specialist who helps overworked, stressed-out, high achieving men and women resolve their chronic health conditions so they can achieve their health and wealth potential. In private practice for 24 years as a Health and Energy Coach, Lidia utilizes her "Capacity Principle™" of Conscious Leadership and Success to help activate the energetic potential of her clients so they can Reclaim Their Health, Regain Their Energy and Refine Their Power. Lidia supports clients with serious health conditions including anxiety, arthritis, auto-immune conditions, cancer, concussions/brain injuries, COPD, heart and stroke conditions and injuries. Lidia's Apona Healing Method provides a step-by-step process to guide clients through the process of healing, so they stay focused, on-track, and Centered, Connected and Conscious™, the 3 keys to unlocking the power to heal and achieving one's mission and potential. Lidia was born with her own chronic health conditions. Through an incredible journey starting at the age 10, Lidia healed her serious health conditions and now loves sharing her experience, knowledge and wisdom with others. It was through spiritual guidance and connection in dreams, that Lidia was guided to utilize the powerful healing modalities of reiki and macrobiotics, to heal herself and support others. What Lidia is most passionate about is empowering Conscious Leaders to feel secure and confident in their knowing that they can turn any crisis or situation into success and activate human potential to Turn Lead Into Gold. Lidia is the creator of The Apona Healing Method™, the Chronic Health Breakthrough Program™ and the Turn Stress Into Success: 3 Steps To Regain Your Energy and Reclaim Your Power™ program. Lidia also shares her passions as a Speaker, Thought Leader and an Award Winning International Best-Selling Author, as part of the book "Navigating The Clickety-Clack: How to Live a Peace-Filled Life in A Seemingly Toxic World."

To Contact Lidia, Please visit www.AponaHealingMethod.com
or e-mail Lidia: Lidia@AponaHealingArts.com

14

SANDRA JOY LARATONDA

DO YOU DEFINE YOUR MONEY STORY OR DOES YOUR MONEY STORY DEFINE YOU?

*I*t was a gorgeous, sunny morning. I stretched and rolled out of bed, still wiping the sleep from my eyes. "I'd better check my bank account to see if that payment cleared," I thought as I reached for my cell phone. My body slumped upon seeing the balance in my account, $24.00. I knew I had more bills to pay. My mind started its deep dive into lack and self-admonishment; the type of energy that prevents you from achieving your money goals. When I started to lose confidence in myself, my issues with lack of money increased. It's a natural side effect of lowering your energy to a place where lack and struggle live.

Everyone has a uniquely personal experience with money. Whether you came from a family that constantly struggled to put food on the table or a home where money was plentiful, you have defined yourself through a money story; a money story that is probably not yours to begin with. Your knowledge and definition of money and how you handle it comes from *this* money story. Dr. Summer J. Caffrey, a dear friend of mine, put this into perspective perfectly when she said, "Financially successful people have stopped reading their money story and started writing it instead." Which one are you, the reader or the writer?

When I was a teenager, my father, a financial planner, took me to the bank to open my first checking and savings account. I was taught to deposit my money, spend the bare minimum I needed to spend, and save the rest. This was how he handled his finances, so I should handle mine the same way. I didn't realize that I was being programmed with deep-seated money beliefs that said my self-worth was directly proportional to the amount of money I had. As a child, I remember wanting to have the latest popular toy and being denied it because it was deemed "too expensive" by my parents. I didn't understand because my friends, who I knew did not have as much money as my family did, received the toy that I wanted so badly to have. My family did not go on vacations to the beach (or anywhere else for that matter) as my friend's families did. Short day trips to local attractions were the extent of the vacations we went on. I remember being envious of my friends and the opportunities they had that I did not. Even in high school, I had to raise my own money for school trips, and if I did not raise enough on my own, I did not go.

I realized when I got older that my parents had their own money stories. They were raised by depression-era parents. This made a huge difference in my parents' view of money. I remember my grandfather saving everything to reuse. We would go to the local bakery, and when we got home, I would watch him meticulously wrap the bakery box string around a beach ball-sized sphere to which he added every piece of string that crossed his path. I don't know who could possibly need that much string, but he had it, just in case. My mother repeated this pattern with rubber bands, twist ties, and grocery bags. These patterns of lack and scarcity that were programmed into my grandparents also affected my parents' money story, which, in turn, affected my money story. Except, I went the opposite way of my parents' pattern.

When I had the chance, I would spend money. I would spend it on anything I wanted because I felt that being denied things in my youth gave me the right to spend my money how I saw fit. It was a blatant show to my parents that they no longer had control of my life or my finances. That attitude fit the rebellious young adult that I was, but it was no friend to my bank account. My spending habits created the need for a second job to support my rebellious spending. I worked 70+ hour weeks in low-paying jobs, and I was trapped in a vicious cycle. Eventually, I decided that something had to change. I agreed to my parents' money story and pursued a college degree and a safe career choice to better my financial position.

My plan failed. I continued to struggle financially. I made ends meet as always and looking in from the outside, it looked like I was prosperous. I spent years, decades in fact, struggling with money management. It was a roller coaster of emotion. There were times when money was flowing endlessly to me and times where money was flowing endlessly away from me. This tug-of-war with money finally stopped when I started looking at my patterns and the energy surrounding them.

Becoming aware of these generational patterns is extremely important because you have the power to stop them and create new, healthy, abundance-filled money patterns. This is especially important if you have children because you have the power to ensure that negative money stories no longer exist. You can teach your children, your siblings, or anyone who is willing to listen about creating financial abundance by releasing self-limiting beliefs. If you have not had a mindset shift surrounding your money story, you can bet that your children have their own negative money story that needs healing. You can begin healing by taking a self-inventory of your money mindset.

The first things I looked at were my self-limiting beliefs surrounding money. I believed that money was scarce, that I had to work hard for it, that money and struggle went hand in hand, that I would never have enough money, and that people who did have money were selfish, greedy, and unwilling to help others without it benefitting them in some way. My money beliefs list went on and on. When I finally sat back and looked at it, every single definition I created around money was negative. Every. Single. One.

I used to shop my fears away. When I became uncomfortable, when something was bothering me, I used retail therapy to fix it. Except, I wasn't fixing anything. I was just continuing a new, unhealthy money story. It was easy enough to get caught up in shopping my worries away. It was instant gratification—a dopamine hit to assuage the pain I refused to deal with. If I had a fight with my boyfriend, I also had a new pair of shoes. It became a game of self-soothing behavior versus credit card balance. I was stuck in that money story for years.

I don't know the exact moment things changed for me, but it was after I was married and had our first child. My husband and I were constantly pouring money into home improvement projects. That was our drug of choice. We could rationalize it because we were adding value to our home. After all, it would come back to us tenfold, right? Wrong. We ended up selling that home for $30k less than we paid for it, not counting the $50k of home improvements we poured into the place for a total loss of $80k. Talk about a wake-up call. We had to fix this.

The first step to changing your mindset around all things money is to take a look into your personal beliefs and the ones that have been passed down to you generationally. It is never money that is the problem. It is the beliefs you assign to money that keep you in lack or abundance. This is a difficult thing to grasp, especially for women. Let's take a look to the past for some clarity.

As long as history has been recorded, women have had one role, to birth and raise children. This role expanded into providing care for not only the children but the family unit as well. Men have traditionally been the breadwinners. Men were raised to be the mighty hunters who provided their kills for food, clothing, and even tools. As society advanced and long-distance trade was established, it was men who took goods to marketplaces and earned wages for their families. Women provided their skills by creating things for men to sell. If a woman lost her husband, her sole source of support, she was in dire straits. She had to earn a wage to keep her children fed and clothed and was often given the worst of the worst of jobs with a wage that was next to nothing. Women sometimes had no choice and resorted to prostitution to earn a decent enough wage to survive. Fast forward to modern times, and women are still struggling to earn an equal wage.

Our ancestral lines are full of struggle, lack, poverty, and strife surrounding money. No wonder we find ourselves struggling financially. We have been programmed to struggle, even during this lifetime, because some of our self-limiting beliefs are instilled in us from our families. If you grew up in poverty, witnessing the struggle to have even the basic necessities, you might have a belief that money is a negative thing that brings pain and grief. Maybe you have the mindset to step out of poverty and create a better life for yourself. You have achieved this, with a nice home, fancy car, latest electronics, etc. —but you still struggle with money and are able to live just within your means but can never seem to get to the next level.

You may have even experienced your family trying to hold you back from success because of their limited beliefs about money. Their financial situation has become comfortable for them, and they are afraid of the unknown, even if that unknown helps them take a step out of their comfort zone to achieve financial success. Oftentimes, people will pull others back down to their comfort level because their sense of community, their tribe, is being threatened. It becomes easier for them to chastise those with money and remain firmly rooted in their limiting beliefs than to step out of their comfort zone and change their situation. In fact, people may allow themselves to achieve just enough to step out of their comfort zone for the next level of success, but; they stop there because their negative money mindset still holds them back.

I know a young man who job hopped from warehouse shift work to warehouse shift work simply because his father, mother, and brother all worked low-paying warehouse jobs. He was offered a position that he had the skills for, which provided a handsome salary, much more than he was making on shift work. For no valid reason, he refused the job and chose to stay in lack and struggle. He continued to live paycheck to paycheck because that is where his comfort level was. This is just one example of how people can keep themselves stuck in a poverty mindset.

You might know someone who constantly plays the lottery hoping to hit it big and solve all of their money problems, or maybe you know someone who depends on government subsidies for years and probably will for the rest of their lives. These types of people are stuck in negative money patterns that they will never get out of because they refuse to see the real reasons behind their money problems. The REAL reason behind all of your money problems is YOU. Yes, that seems harsh, and I'm sure that you are thinking of every single reason that is *not* you right now to prove me wrong. The thing is, YOU are the only one who can change your money situation. It *can* be changed, and all it takes is the shifting of some limited beliefs.

If you find yourself struggling with money, there are ways to end that struggle once and for all. By this point, you may be asking yourself how to change your energy around money. First, you can start with the words you use to describe it. Do you talk about money in a positive way? Really listen to the words you use when you discuss anything to do with money. When you pay a bill do you grumble and complain about the money going out to cover that payment, or are you thankful that you have the money to meet your obligation? Do you release that money with fear that you will struggle to get enough for next time or with faith that you will have all of the money that you need? The energy you release around money is the energy you will call back to yourself.

I had been working with energies and self-limiting beliefs for a few years when I came to this realization. There are so many energies surrounding money, but we only need to focus on one, the energy of abundance. In reality, there is an unlimited amount of money available for you, and you just need to align yourself with the energy of abundance for it to start showing up in your life. The way that you do that is to look at the way you interact with money. Notice the energy that you are putting out every time you spend or receive money because that is the exact energy that returns to you.

How often have you subconsciously reinforced a negative money belief based on a stereotype? I drive a Mercedes Benz. Stop. What did you just think about when you read that sentence? It was ten years old when I bought it, yet people have strong opinions, nonetheless. I immediately received comments like "It must be nice to be able to afford that" or "I have to go get one now to keep up with you" and "You look good in that car"—among countless other well-meaning but negative comments. Here's the thing, people negatively judge others by what they have, whether they realize it or not. My husband just traded in his Ford Fusion with over 152k miles on it and purchased a five year old Mercedes Benz. The moment I told my mother what kind of car he purchased, she immediately rolled her eyes and said, "Well, good for him." There it was, money judgement in full effect. In reality, his "new" car was priced far below the price she paid for her brand new Hyundai SUV crossover, yet the "better than you" or "showing off" judgement was still there.

If you haven't noticed, we are in a pandemic and a financial crisis. People are mired in lack and fear. Some people struggled hard with job loss, and government assistance barely covered their basic needs. Meanwhile, our family had our best financial year ever because we shifted our mindset on what making money during a pandemic looked like. Instead of becoming trapped in fear, we focused on all the abundance that was surrounding us. As the saying goes, there's money all over the floor, you just have to know how to pick it up. I shifted my brick-and-mortar business to an online business, and I supported my husband in his real estate work and encouraged him with investing in new stock trading accounts. I also took courses that would further my career while I had all that extra time at home. I invested in myself and my family. Even when things became financially scary for us, we refused to be stuck in the lack and fear mindset that the media was spewing. We had the right mindset, and that was an essential part of being financially responsible and making it through the forced shutdowns unscathed.

Many people were successful in starting their own businesses from home during this time with little to no money and creating a solid financial future. However, others let themselves become stuck in fear and lack and are now worse off than they were before this whole thing started. As I write this, there is a rent crisis, and people owe up to a year or more of back rent for their homes because they chose to use their government rent subsidies for other things that they did not truly need. The societal image that is force-fed to us is that our self-worth and importance are defined by the things we have, the latest phone, the nicest car, the newest fashion, and that if we are poor, we are owed a living. Very little emphasis is placed on actual financial accountability and responsibility. It is this mindset that traps people in lack and fear and prevents abundance from ever finding them.

You don't know what you don't know, and your concept of having and not having money is most likely skewed. You may be under the impression that having lots of money and buying expensive things makes you selfish. That wealthy people should give money away to the less fortunate. No one considers that everything is created by something else. Let's consider yachts. Yachts are expensive luxury items. When someone buys a yacht, they are paying for the manufacturing of every piece of that yacht. Thousands of people who had a hand in creating that yacht, from the mechanics to the napkins, have received a wage for their part in its creation. The person who purchased that yacht has not just paid the dealership but also every single person who had a hand in its creation. You might be thinking, well, that's not fair because some people who worked on that yacht are barely making ends meet. Yet, those same people who are barely making ends meet can own their own yacht one day if they want to. Mindset is everything. First, you have to have the desire to change. Next, you must recognize the opportunities the universe provides. Then you have to act on them; because ideas without action become regrets.

How do you define your relationship with money? Is it readily available to you? Is it reliable? Can you depend on it always being there? Is it hard to get? Are earning and keeping money a struggle? The way you define your relationship with money is the way money shows up (or doesn't) in your life. It's really as simple as that. Once you actually understand how you think about money and your relationship with it, you can begin to heal and release those self-limiting beliefs that have held you back for far too long.

If you constantly think negative thoughts about money, you will constantly find yourself in a state of lack. Lack causes struggle, struggle creates bitterness, the energy of bitterness becomes your money mindset. Are you noticing the pattern? Do you see the areas of negative talk that you can adjust? What if you thanked the universe for providing this money so you could pay your debts? What if your outlook on money shifted into the positive, where you became thankful for every penny you had and celebrated all money that comes to you as well as all money you release?

Keeping a gratitude journal can be very helpful in your mindset shift. Every one of my spiritual teachers has used journaling and gratitude in some form. The common thread through all of them is that writing something down and being unabashedly grateful for the moments and things that happen (or have yet to happen) in your life does one thing: raises your energetic vibration. When you raise your vibration, you are able to call in abundance more easily. Having a higher energetic vibration means being aligned to something in the higher energetic realms where abundance resides. You must shift your thoughts to positive, abundance-filled thoughts to see any kind of results that you are dedicated to manifesting.

Weak moments do happen, and you shouldn't give up your goal. Shifting your mindset around money is not a once and done thing. You may notice yourself falling back into old patterns, and that's ok. The biggest achievement is that you recognized it this time. Whether it is spending money for a holiday, people-pleasing purchases, or self-soothing spending habits, being self-aware of your emotional ties to money is the first step to shifting your mindset to a more stable financial ground.

Helping people achieve this outcome is especially important to me because I know firsthand how helpless it felt to be in those dire straits with no way out (or so I thought). My clients have expressed how grateful they are to me that I have shed light on the self-limiting behaviors they have been living with and helped them create a plan to shift their negative money stories to ones of financial abundance. I explored their money stories, dug deep, and revealed the patterns that held them back. I helped them rewrite their money stories to ones of success that were focused on abundance. Shifting your mindset around money also creates shifts in other areas as well. My clients have had breakthroughs in relationships, self-confidence, and overall happiness.

Dedication to your mindset is everything. Stop embracing self-doubt and defining your worth by a job or possessions. Release the guilt passed on from prior generations along with the belief that your current financial status defines your ability to achieve wealth. Go deep into yourself and heal your ancestral lines. Be conscious of the stories that you tell yourself about money. Be dedicated to your energy consciousness work, visualization, and the energy you are releasing to the universe. Shift your thoughts from limited to limitless possibilities and let go of the excuses you hold on to that keep you stuck. If you continue to think that you are doing the best you can and don't step out of your comfort zone, then you are short-changing yourself and missing great opportunities for abundance to show up in your life.

If you would like to explore your money story on a deeper level with me and conquer your current fears, please reach out and contact me. It would be my honor to walk with you.

Where to Find Me:
Website: http://www.SandraJoy.com
Email: Sandra@SandraJoy.com
Insta: @SandraJoySol
TikTok: @SandraJoySol
Clubhouse: @SandraJoySol

ABOUT THE AUTHOR
SANDRA JOY LARATONDA

Sandra Joy is the founder and CEO of Healing Realms, LLC and Sandra Joy, LLC. She embraces the new energy consciousness of Earth and guides others to embrace this energy to connect and thrive in their soul purpose.

She is an Adult Indigo with a deep connection to Indigo, Crystal, and Diamond Children as well as a highly intuitive clairsentient. She is a Lightworker certified with Hands of Light, a Master Usui Reiki Practitioner, a Crystal and Color Energies Expert, a certified Hypnotherapist, certified Oracle Card reader, and a 20 year activator of Indigo and Crystal Children.

Her purpose in this lifetime is to connect with people who want to learn how to harness the power of their energy system and thrive in their soul's purpose. She lives in Pennsylvania on a small farm with her husband, son, daughter, and many animals.

Website: SandraJoy.com
Facebook Group:
www.facebook.com/groups/UnTameYourSoul
Instagram:
www.Instagram.com/The.Sandra.Joy

15

SARAH BRIGID BROWN
THE DAY THE UNIVERSE PUT ME ON THE RIGHT PATH

*L*ife as I knew it suddenly stopped back in 2008 when I was diagnosed with a massive slipped disc at the base of my spine. At the time, I was working extremely hard as a translator and language trainer and juggling all my work responsibilities with looking after our three children and keeping our home clean and tidy. My body was telling me that something had to change and fast...

When my doctor told me that my physical pain and crippling condition might be related to my thoughts, beliefs, and emotional state, I realized that I needed to open my eyes to my reality.

What I saw was scary! In my quest to make sure that my family and I had a secure, loving home environment, I had put my own needs to one side. In fact, I had no idea what my own needs were.

I had got used to managing, aka controlling, most, if not all, of our family life, and would regularly be up until the early hours, tidying up and washing the dishes long after everyone else had gone to bed. I was pushing past the mental and physical exhaustion, day after day, until it was no longer possible.

Lying in my bed, suffering from the most excruciating pain, I wasn't sure of the next step I should take, and I became aware of how unsure I was about most things. What had happened for me to become so unaligned?

Growing up, I had always been the responsible one, the person who knew what she wanted and who would do everything in her power to make things happen. I was brought up thinking that I had to work hard to better myself and that the only way to do this was to listen to what other people were saying and doing and follow their example.

What I didn't realize at the time was that I was slowly dimming my light to fit in with society.

On the occasions when I was 'just me', I remember being told things like 'You can't do that' or 'Who do you think you are?'. As a highly sensitive empath (words that I had no idea existed back then), I took this at face value and started to adapt my behavior and my life to what other people wanted and expected from me.

There were times when I would let my real self out, like when I moved away to go to university or when I spent a year in France as part of my degree, but it often seemed much easier for me to just follow the traditional path of settling down, having kids and a good job.

This worked until 2006 when the first signs of health problems started to show up. Anyone who knows me will tell you that I am petite. The reason I am telling you this is that I put on a lot of weight during two of my three pregnancies, and my back suffered for it. So, when I started to have a stiff back or a trapped nerve, I just thought that it was because of that and would go to the doctor's for medication (as you do).

As I had learnt to be strong and just keep going, never once did it occur to me that my body was trying to tell me something. That is, until one fateful day in August 2008.

My husband, children, and I were on holiday in a beautiful part of the south of France, just a few minutes' drive from the Mediterranean Sea. We had finally been able to find somewhere that all of us would like – a family campsite with activities for the kids, surrounded by nature, a swimming pool for us all, and easy access to the beach. We had decided to camp for the first time, and I personally couldn't wait to get there after a difficult few months at work.

I had recently been promoted to project manager and had to manage a team of six people. Deadlines were short, some team members weren't pulling their weight, and I didn't have the support I needed from my line manager. I just did what I knew how to – try and handle things on my own, work long hours and ignore what my gut was telling me.

It is no secret that we often get ill on holiday, simply because we start to relax and our body can let its defenses down. This is what happened to me. On the third morning of our holiday, I woke up, went to sit up in the tent, and felt the most excruciating pain, like someone had cut me in two. It was so bad I had to lie back down. I waited a few minutes, tried again, and the same thing happened. I knew that something wasn't right and that it would take more than just a Nurofen, hot water bottle, and rest to feel better.

There was no other solution than to cut the holiday short and drive home so that I could see my doctor as quickly as possible. He diagnosed a trapped nerve, gave me painkillers for a week, and told me to rest. I could do that. The only thing is that after that week, I was still in as much pain as before, and to cut a long story short, after several weeks of medication and physiotherapy, I was diagnosed with a massive slipped disc. The only solution was to operate, as my right leg was already more or less paralyzed, and if I didn't act quickly, I would run the risk of ending up disabled for the rest of my life.

I will never forget that day. It felt like my whole world had caved in – which it had, unbeknownst to me at the time. Panic and fear set in big time. What does the operation entail? What are the risks? Will I ever be able to walk properly again? How will we all cope while I am convalescing? And worse still, what happens if the operation doesn't work and I am left paralyzed?

That's when the little voice inside me started whispering – there has to be another way.

That other way appeared in the form of reading a book that explains the mind-body connection, going to see a psycho-energetic therapist, and being treated by an osteopath. All recommended by my doctor.

After a few months of professional help, I was already in a better place. The threat of having surgery to physically remove what had caused me excruciating pain had disappeared, and I had started to understand everything that had led me to this point in my life. During my sessions with my therapist, I was able to identify the times when I had shut myself off from my emotions, put others first, controlled what was happening to me and others, and basically become disconnected from who I really am.

It was time to reclaim my inner power, so I resigned from my job, started my own business as a language service provider, and very quickly realized that this was the path meant for me. I loved the freedom it had given me. I loved being able to choose what felt right for me, and most of all, I vowed to pay it forward one day.

Helping both adults to improve their language skills and companies to increase their international presence is a wonderful thing to do. But after a few years of being in business, I started to feel restless and knew there was a lot more for me to provide to the world. That's when I remembered the vow I had made and how learning about my past behaviors had given me the confidence to break through my doubts and fears, and free myself from other people's judgment.

The question was: How can I help others do the same thing? I felt like I didn't have all the skills and knowledge that I needed, so I connected to my angels and intuition for guidance. One morning, I sat down in front of my computer and started searching for ideas. It wasn't long before I came across coaching, and a few minutes later (literally!), I had found the perfect training course for me, sent an email, and been accepted as part of the next intake a few weeks later!

Since then, I have also trained in several different modalities as my desire to go even deeper with my clients grows. I have learnt what it takes to heal my past and create a soul-aligned life, and my purpose is to guide others to do the same.

Looking back on my journey so far, I can see many blessings in my struggles, and I would like to share some of them with you:

1) Our mind can be our best friend or our worst enemy. It can tell us that we are the greatest person on earth or that we will never be enough. It has the power to influence how we treat our body, how we show up in life, and how we feel about ourselves, every day, every hour, every minute. We can let it work for us or allow it to work against us.

2) Our soul is always whispering to us, always. It is up to us to tune in or not. To trust what it is saying or not. I learnt this the hard way, which led to my body stopping me in my tracks back in 2008. I think that was probably my greatest lesson to come from all that happened back then, to listen to my soul. Since I have been listening, I have had such fantastic experiences, including being awarded the prize for most promising solopreneur in France, manifesting our house, flying across the world to Northern California to take part in a women's awakening retreat, and now being one of the authors of this wonderful book!

3) Our past holds the keys to set us free, whether or not we know it. So many of us have experienced heartache, disappointment, and rejection and would rather try and forget what has happened. I get it, I really do, because that's what I did for nearly forty years. What you need to know is that your body remembers – everything, every little detail, every emotion, every desire. Nobody teaches us this when we are growing up, and even when we are adults. We are led to believe

that we can talk ourselves into anything, that our aches and pains can go away by taking medicine, that mental intelligence is so much more important than emotional intelligence. And we all buy into it until the pain gets too heavy. If we are lucky, we find someone to take our hand and show us a better way.

My way of paying it forward is to take what I have learnt during my trainings and share it with my clients. The saying goes that knowledge is power, and by sharing my knowledge with you, I aim to empower you to birth your best self. So, how do I do this?

I use the power of NLP (neuro-linguistic programming) to help you reframe past experiences, thoughts, and beliefs. NLP can help us improve our communication with ourselves and other people, access a positive state such as confidence or calm, and gain clarity on our vision, life purpose, and values. Some of the results my clients have achieved are a better understanding of their loved ones, new life being breathed into their relationship with their partner, being less of a perfectionist, and allowing others to support them so that they no longer feel like they have to do everything on their own.

Another great tool I bring into my coaching practice is EFT (emotional freedom technique). Whenever we experience a traumatic event (it could be a single event or something that is repeated), our body registers it somewhere, together with the emotions that we felt at that particular moment in time. As the majority of us are extremely resilient, even if we don't admit it, we can often tend to 'just get on with life' – until life decides to remind us of a particular event, in the form of a limiting belief, lack of self-esteem, self-confidence and/or self-love, for example. Depending on what we experienced and on our individual capacity to heal, a "normal" coaching session may not be enough to accept this, process this, and move forwards. This is often when I introduce my clients to EFT.

It has been found that EFT leads to a 68% decrease in physical problems, such as pain and disease, and a 45% decrease in psychological problems, like anxiety, depression, fear, and phobia.

Here are some of the things my clients have shared with me just after an EFT session:

"I feel great. It's really extraordinary! It's like you've removed a lot of thorns from my side, and I feel really free and relaxed."

"I feel aligned and powerful."

"Thank you for this leap forward! I've finally understood the connection between a childhood experience and what's holding me back today."

"My heart has opened, and I feel relieved. I have a clearer vision of the situation now."

Working with and on our emotions is, in my opinion, one of THE keys to healing. I personally believe that emotional healing goes hand in hand with energy healing, as all emotions are energy moving through the body (energy in motion (e-motion)). There are many different ways to improve your health and life with energy healing, and I currently use three of them.

1) IET® (integrated energy therapy) is a little-known modality with far-reaching effects. As mentioned by its founder, Stevan Thacker, it is a powerful energy therapy system that gets the "issues out of your tissues" for good! IET uses nine primary energy locations in the body, including the seven main chakras and major organs of the body. Universal energy is channeled by the therapist, who then applies gentle pressure on the nine points to help release the energy of emotions stored in the cellular memories of the body. This technique has been summed up as *integrating the pain of the past into the power of the present to bring about the joy of the future.*

2) Chakra balancing or releasing blockages in our main energy centers. As mentioned above, IET can help with this, as can sound therapy (see point 3 below). The way that I have chosen to balance chakras is through guided meditation, visualization, and chanting mantras. This is part of what I teach in my online and face-to-face

group workshops, designed to introduce people to the role the chakras play in our physical, emotional, and mental well-being.

3) Sound therapy with Tibetan singing bowls. This is a new modality for me as I write and one I had the pleasure of discovering during a yoga retreat in summer 2021. I loved it so much that I trained to use the bowls to help balance our chakras and cleanse our aura. Experts in sound healing state that each part of our body has its own frequency and that the vibratory frequencies of the cells in our body can be harmonized thanks to this type of therapy. I can tell you, for having been on the receiving end of a sound bath and the vibrations of Tibetan singing bowls placed on my body, that it really works. I could feel and even sometimes see low-frequency energy being dissolved, leaving me feeling much lighter afterwards and helping me have a much clearer vision of my future.

Part of this vision is the coaching programs that I offer: Learning to Heal Your Past and Birthing Your Best Self. Learning to Heal Your Past is designed to help you accept your past and empower yourself to move forwards. With Birthing Your Best Self, we take what you have learnt about your past and build on that to explore your desires, needs, and values, work on self-love and forgiveness, and find your passion, create a new sense of confidence, and step into your personal power.

I now know, in my heart of hearts, that all of my life experiences have led me to the perfect place for me. A place where I have the privilege of being the first person that people have dared to bare their soul to. A place where those same people feel safe, heard, and understood. A place where I am truly and authentically me.

I would like to finish by sharing a quote from The Alchemist by Paulo Coelho, as I feel it sums up my mission and life purpose.

"Courage in the path is what makes the path manifest itself."

What will be the next step on yours?

ABOUT THE AUTHOR
SARAH BRIGID BROWN

Sarah Brigid Brown is a bilingual life transition coach, with a passion to share her knowledge and wisdom, helping sensitive, empathic men and women over 40 develop their confidence, balance their energies and emotions, and become happier people for it.

She does this by accompanying them on a journey to heal their past, reconnect to their inner child and love themselves enough to create a brighter and better future. This leads them to step into their life purpose, as they've reconnected to their heart and fundamentally changed how they see themselves.

Sarah knows exactly what it's like to embrace your purpose, as she went from being a people pleaser, always wanting to control everything, afraid to speak up and totally disconnected from who she REALLY was, to a passionate coach, teacher and guide, in love with life and her life, following her calling to help as many people as possible, embracing all her imperfections and believing in a future where love and community reign.

Sarah's approach is very holistic. She's a qualified EFT Practitioner, Performance Coach with NLP, IET Practitioner, New Paradigm MDT Master Practitioner and recently trained to be a Singing Bowl Sound Therapist.

What she loves more than anything else is letting her intuition guide her towards the modalities that would best serve each individual person.

Website: www.so-free.life
YouTube: www.youtube.com/c/SoFreeCoaching

16

SHANDRA NICOLE SHULTZ
THE RISE OF THE PHOENIX: MY JOURNEY THROUGH ADDICTION

"*9* years, 8 months, and 14 days (as of the time of writing this)"— that is how long I have been in sober recovery. This is my story of overcoming addiction and the Spiritual journey to heal and transcend it.

By the time I was seventeen years old, I was "a full-blown drug addict". I had not intended to become so, and honestly, I did not even realize that I was until it was too late. My doctors had diagnosed me in 1997 at fourteen with Polycystic Ovarian Syndrome and Dysmenorrhea. In other words, "I had chronic cysts on my ovaries as well as a host of other issues that come along and severely painful periods". Being that my Gynecologist and Primary Care doctors were men, they did the pertinent thing of that time and gave me a script of Vicodin with unlimited refills, which happened to be every month it seemed, and sent me on my merry way.

What I did not know then and sadly took almost twenty years to realize was that my pain was not just physical; it was both mental and emotional too. It had become a triple threat of pain, and I was never taught how to handle it other than to run away from, shove it down or cover it up with something that would take away said pain. I would remain actively addicted for the next twelve years until I was twenty-nine, during that time becoming a single mom while dealing with mental illness, death, overdosing several times, surviving severe abuse as well as kidnapping and many attempts at suicide.

Let me take a step back and discuss how I became addicted. Many believed it was the inability to simply have the "willpower to control myself" when partaking in whatever it was that I was doing. Whether that was reading (somethings over 300+ books a year, many times forgoing sleep just to finish my book), food, gambling, multimedia, drugs, alcohol, working, pleasure, pretty much if you could name it, I had some level of addiction to it or abused it in some way at one point in my life or another. I was a high functioning addict, and many did not even realize or believe it was possible for me to be addicted to these things. One might have believed that the process of quitting something or controlling myself when doing so was to be an easy task as they could not see my addictions. I assure you, however, for me, it was not an easy task at all. While for some it is, for me and many others, having "willpower to quit" was something like the obsession of searching for the lost treasure of the Aztecs or the city of Atlantis—no matter how hard one tries, they just could not seem to find it, and yet they will never give up trying. It becomes a process of running in circles, doing the same thing repeatedly, yet believing that someday they will finally be successful or have a different outcome—truly the definition of insanity.

Many individuals are unknowingly shown a form of addiction while growing up, and I was no different. My mom was a workaholic, not that I knew this at the time. All I knew was it felt like she never stopped working and, in her own words, called herself a "natural speed freak". I suppose to some extent, so was my dad. I did not recognize it as such because back then, his being gone was "normal" for me as I was told that was the case with all truck-drivers, however, it created a large abandonment wound.

I remember at one point in my childhood, my mom would consume up to six pots of coffee daily and yet could still go to sleep like a baby by 10pm every night. As a workaholic, when she finally did stop working for the week, she was so exhausted, and while she did her best to keep up with me and hide her exhaustion from me, I realize now just how exhausted she was—except it wasn't so much physical exhaustion, though I am sure there was some of that as she did work up to four jobs and go to school full time at one point in my childhood, but instead a combination of physical, mental and emotional exhaustion.

Growing up, my mom was my hero. I remember writing essays about how I wanted to be just like my "mommy" when I grew up. I didn't mean so much at that time physically and emotionally like her. No, what I meant was that I wanted to be like the strong and resilient woman she modeled for me who stuck by her family through thick and thin and loved me unconditionally. The type of woman who, no matter how many times things tried to knock her down, she never gave up and always kept going. She tells me now that I have a positivity and a light about me the likes of which she has never seen. However, the only way I was able to learn to hold my light this way was from learning as a child from her. I saw a strength of perseverance in my mom even in the most daunting of times, which I would later gain for myself as well, through my own challenging times. Sometime between the time my dad died in 2004, and when we were hit head-on by a drunk driver in 2005, that light slowly started to fade in her. I can say that in recent years, while I did healing for myself and my ancestral line, I have seen shifts in her, and that light has started to reemerge. A truer testament to the power of healing I feel does not exist.

In many ways, my mom was a single mom. While married to my dad my entire childhood until he passed when I was 21, my dad traveled for work and was gone often. As such, she was my primary model of how to become an adult. One thing my mom modeled for me was to "compartmentalize your life experiences so that you lock away the nasty, ugly ones and ALL the emotions surrounding them," as that was how she learned to cope with the intense level of abandonment and trauma she had lived through.

Fortunately for me, I did not take on this trait. Instead, I learned severe emotional dysregulation from other places. I read a lot of romance novels and other fiction stories growing up, which I often became completely immersed in and used to escape the pain and all I felt on an emotional level for as long as I could remember. From these books and from television, too, I would imagine myself as if I were the characters and would get lost for hours in the rich fantasy life that I had created. Sometimes I would become so lost that I would lose all sense of time and completely forget what else I had to do in life. My school life suffered especially, however, and I became an expert at procrastination.

I was highly sensitive and emotional as a child and teenager. I can remember my dad was often triggered by my level of emotionality. While I didn't know it then, he was not allowed to have BIG feelings or really any feelings because he was "a boy, and they had to suck it up and be a man"; sad signs of the toxic patriarchy in which he was raised. My dad repeated the same things to me in many ways that his own father did to him. As children, we are little sponges and take in everything like a computer, storing information with no context or the ability to have discernment. This means that our existence and experiences create this level of normalcy which for many would never have seemed "normal" and as such when we become adults (which actually happens at the age of 25 with normal cognitive or "brain" development), we often act out the very same "stories" that we lived in growing up.

My pain started in childhood, as it has for many others. While I had two parents who both loved and wanted me (in the ways they knew how), they were also very wounded from their own childhood and beyond and were operating from that space when I was born. Additionally, my parents came from two completely different walks of life. My mom was raised in a Catholic household in the North-Eastern part of the United States though she eventually became a born-again Christian Hippie, and my dad was raised in a strict Southern Baptist post-war Military family in deep south Arkansas. Being as they were both born between the tail end of WWII and the Korean War, they were raised with very different values and had completely different upbringings. While my dad was raised with the "Nuclear Family", my mom was passed around in the foster systems. Both suffered severe abuse, which was "normal" back then, and this colored how they raised me.

I never realized as a young person how much their backgrounds could affect me, both positively and negatively. While my mom valued Independence and Feminine freedom, my dad was a Vietnam Veteran who longed for a family of his own that he could love, protect and provide for in the ways he had both had loved and at times hated growing up. My mom worked and did not feel she could rely on anyone outside herself before meeting my dad. She had become the "ultimate" single woman. Then they had me, and everything changed. It was like a light switch turned on, and suddenly, they were both living out their wounds of childhood and adolescence in their relationship with each other and with me.

I do not remember most of my childhood before I was six, and I am sure that part of that is due to the trauma that I endured as a child. I was raped by the teenage son of a family friend at that age, as well as had several injuries, which included biting my tongue almost clean off on my sixth birthday and severe chickenpox during the Christmas of 1989, which required me to be secluded from everyone except my mom because she was immune.

My dad traveled a lot as a Salesman in the eighties, so I did not get to see him much, which, as we know, can often lead to abandonment wounds and relational issues between the parent and child. When I was seven, my dad became a long-haul truck driver and ended up being gone even more than he had in my early childhood. To be exact, he was gone 332 days a year. It is no wonder that our relationship was strained and rocky as my undeveloped brain was not able to understand logic nor reason and simply thought he no longer wanted me or that I had done something to cause him to leave me for so long. It did not matter to my newly developing ego that my dad would bring me gifts or record tapes with stories, all she knew was that the daddy she longed for was not around and that he chose to stay away. Of course, decades later, when I started doing the emotional and spiritual work of healing, I would come to realize that he was doing what he had been taught to do and thought best.

My mom, having gotten fed up with the inconsistency of my dad's paychecks as a Salesman, had given him an ultimatum which consisted of "bring me home a steady check or suffer some unnamed consequence." To this day, I do not know what would have happened had she not received what she desired. However from what I have been told, divorce was on the table and, in fact, had almost happened more than once. This resulted in what I believed at the time to be my dad choosing a high-paying job which was steady money and could fit with his skillset, though it required him to be away from his family and, in truth, to be secluded from life in so many ways. Unfortunately I do not know the truth of why he chose truck driving, he passed before we were able to have those conversations, and well before my gaining the awareness of a healthy adult self. I do know that this affected my dad on a visceral level, however. Not only did his own PTSD from the war become triggered, but deep childhood wounds also seemed to surface, though none of us understood that at the time. In turn, similar wounds became triggered in my mom, and they lived a life separate yet together. Sadly, through their wounding, they also set me up to have similar wounds that I would eventually uncover upon gaining my sobriety.

As with many children today, I found myself bullied most of my adolescence until I graduated high school. I was made to be a pariah by many of my classmates, so much so that they would prank me with large containers of Slim-Fast (an American "weight loss" shake, which NO 10 year old should be drinking, nor do they need to be so worried about their weight) and fake notes from "boys", something now called "Cat-Fishing," to calling me names in front of the whole class or telling me I was too fat to try out of the dance team. The ages of nine to seventeen were horrible for me, and they ended with me being raped and almost killed at a party on my seventeenth birthday. I was tired of the abuse, and for the first time, sadly though not the last, I tried to commit suicide. A "friend" found me mid-dosing and was able to get the pills out of my mouth, and my parents got me in to see a psychiatrist. That was the first time it felt like someone truly listened to me, however, instead of other measures to heal and recover, I was misdiagnosed with bipolar disorder and promptly placed on psychiatric meds. What I had, in fact, was Complex PTSD from all the abuse and trauma I suffered, which included watching my family's episodes of PTSD; my father's from his time during the War and childhood, as well as my mom's from her childhood and adolescence—we were a fucked-up family full of wounds and none of us at that time knew it nor how to proceed healthily with such.

I remember as a kid always feeling like I had to walk on eggshells. I knew my mom loved me unconditionally and that my dad loved me conditionally, so I developed codependent traits to survive living in a household that, to me as a child, always felt unsettled when my dad was home. When I was fourteen, my dad found a local truck driving job that allowed him to be home on weekends, which I both dreaded and loved. My dad was finally home and not gone so often, however, at the same time, we clashed so much because he still saw me as the little girl he had left and not the growing woman I was becoming. Our relationship was at best rocky and at worst downright volatile. We often got in the worst screaming matches, which even led to his being physically abusive with me one time when he kicked me out of the house at 16. Being that I was an "overly emotional teenager," my dad convinced my mom that I was exaggerating, which is where I started to separate from my parents and started disbelieving in myself to some extent.

The next seven years, until my dad passed from cancer in 2004, were the beginning of the rockiest years in my life. It was during this time that I unknowingly became addicted to Vicodin. Then at seventeen, after being raped for the 2nd time in my young life, I found myself with a group of individuals where I finally felt safe, accepted, and like I wasn't the screw up anymore because we were ALL screwed up, and that is what united us. This group introduced me to Ecstasy and Speed, aka Methamphetamine, as well as a host of other drugs and experiences, which allowed me to feel so alive. It was during this time that I also found out my dad had cancer. Instead of including me in everything, my parents told me only "need to know" information, or so it felt to me. The pain I felt was overwhelming, and I did what anyone who was not taught to face the pain and trauma does, I ran away and used anything and everything I could to escape. I had already become so good at it that it was second nature to me. I started running at seventeen and didn't stop until I was twenty-nine. During that time, I went through many abusive relationships, was assaulted by "friends" more times than I can count as I was either too high or too drunk to say "NO" and found myself surviving being kidnapped by a serial rapist.

At twenty-one, just six months after my dad died, I became pregnant with the one and only child I was able to both bring to term and ultimately have. Even this experience was not enough for me to fully quit and get sober. It lasted for eleven months and ended the day my family and I were struck head-on by a drunk driver a mere five weeks post-pregnancy. Gratefully we all survived, though we were never the same again. I lost my sobriety because I did not have the tools to move through everything I was dealing with. This eventually started me on my journey to recovery, however, as I was tired of all the emotional ups and downs, though at that point I did not put two and two together that the drugs might be playing a part in the issue.

I entered a period of my life where I started searching for healing in any way that I could find, from reading books to studying Psychology and getting a degree in it as I thought this would be the thing to help me understand myself—and it did, to an extent. It took me another eight years, sadly, to fully gain my sobriety over drugs and alcohol. In fact, it took an event where I woke up in a stranger's bed after a weekend of partying and finally seeing myself through the eyes of others and asking myself "WHAT THE FUCK?!?!" I was doing with my life, for me to choose me and to start truly healing.

The entire time I was searching, I never thought to look at Spirit or Spiritual healing. I was a nerd who believed in science and had been taught that science was "the way". It wouldn't be until I was thirty-one years old, two years after getting sober, where I suffered another horrific accident which left me without my memory up to the point of the crash (Amnesia), not being able to remember my mom, my kid or the life I had led up to that point, in addition to the inability to read, write, and speak properly, that I would truly find faith and turn to Spirit to heal.

During that time, I found myself continuing to search, though, at that point, I did not remember what I was searching for as I did not remember my addiction. It was not until I found my journals covering the years of my addiction, over twelve-plus years, that I learned who I had been and what all had happened to me. This did not exactly open the flood gates; however, it cracked the dam, and slowly pieces of my life started to trickle back to me. This time, somehow, I had an awareness due to being sober that I needed to make a different choice. It was during this time that I dedicated myself to my sovereign Goddess, the Celtic Brigid, and started the journey to heal my soul as I felt intuitively in my gut that I had been given a second chance at life and that I had best not waste it. Shortly after dedicating myself to Brigid, I met my now husband, who had been living across the street from me for SIX months, and yet even with his garage spot next to mine, I never "saw" him. I believe it was that I was so wounded from my past that I refused to allow myself to do so. You see, he was in the Navy, and the old me would never have even given him a chance after all I lived through with my dad. However, the new me did not remember this and was allowing herself to be led by Spirit, so I jumped. Being with this man, my Bear, as I have come to call him, was the first time in my life that I felt truly loved, safe, and supported by a man (even if I did not fully understand that at that time). He made the decision to support me in my recovery from the injuries that I had suffered during the accident, and because of this, for the first time in my life, I was truly from a non-selfish place able to choose me first and to focus on my healing full-time. I have spent the past seven years being able to return to full health because of this. This is not to say that it was easy—far from it. During this time, my husband was released from active duty and became fully disabled from his injuries sustained during his fourteen years of service.

This allowed us to financially sustain ourselves for some time, which allowed me to dive deeper into the healing I so desperately felt called to find. In 2017 I was at a metaphysical fair and met my now Reiki Master Teacher. This was the beginning of finding my healing and my tribe. I went on that same year to become a Reiki Master Teacher myself, as well as learn countless other modalities, which included learning to enter, read and rewrite my own Akashic Records, connecting with my angels and Spirit teams, and many more. I embraced and studied Shamanism and learned of my "shadow-self". Though skeptical of my ability to ever fully "quiet my mind", I started a daily meditation practice in 2018 and found myself slowly learning to "witness" my thoughts and slowing down in my life.

Unfortunately, I had not done so in a timely enough manner for Spirit as I was still very much making decisions from a place of fear, lack, and scarcity, and in the spring of 2018, we found ourselves homeless. I suffered two accidents, and my husband started having seizures which forced him to stop going to school and truly tested our faith in Spirit. It did not end there as I had two more accidents later that year and realized I had to get out of the line of work I had been in and had to start listening full time to Spirit. During all this, my sobriety was often tested, not by having someone offer me a drink or drugs, no, rather by the sheer amount of crap I was dealing with, and

I wanted nothing but to feel better and run away. When that would arise, I would journal about it, as journaling had become a daily practice too, and I would turn to my guides in meditation to gain support and guidance of where to go next. It was at this point Spirit shifted my focus to the inner world that was showing up for me externally, the shadow-self was rising, and I was entering a "Dark Night of the Soul".

I then learned of a modality that was grounded in spirituality and simple Psychology, it was called The Adult Chair. It allowed me to re-parent myself from a space of compassion, grace and love, coming to understand why my parents were the way they were, that they had just done the best they could, and that they loved me in the ways they knew how. I finally found something that allowed me to heal my wounded parts and become whole again. In 2019 I focused deeply on this task as I knew intuitively it was led by Spirit to allow me to continue the mission of healing my wounded self. I went deep into the shadows, as I was taught to call them through Shamanic practice, and shined the light I had learned to cultivate on the pieces of me that had long been hidden, locked away, or disowned. This is not to say that the work is done, no, instead it taught me that we are as Shrek says, "like onions, we have layers".

In 2020 I was given the opportunity to become certified in The Adult Chair modality as a coach. I leaped on the chance to do so, as I knew that by adding this to everything that I learned regarding the Spiritual realm, I would have an amazing opportunity to teach others how to heal their own shadows and live in their authentic truth, just as I had learned. In a few short years, I turned my life around, and now I felt called to teach others how to do the same. It is with that in mind that I created my business in 2017 called Healings of Light and Love by Shandra. Now I lead others in the ways I had wished I had been guided growing up. I have created a modality called Soul Birth Session ™ in which I guide my clients through a process of unleashing their authentic self, which may be buried under layers of limiting beliefs, trauma, unknown wounds, toxic thought patterns, and negative self-talk. By taking my clients on a journey of rediscovering their inner child, reprogramming outdated beliefs, and reconnecting with the parts of themselves that they misplaced or disowned, I guide my clients from run-down and ragged to embodied and empowered.

I have created the Building A WOO You Academy ™, which will be a place for individuals looking to learn the tools to connect with their intuition, Spirit, and Source and to feel divinely guided to live their best life. This space will offer classes in subjects such as intuition, divination, shamanic shadow-work, and so much more, coming Winter 2021. I am the Creatrix of the "I Got the Woo! ™" Community on Facebook as a way for those desiring to connect with their tribe and learn how to embrace their woo in a safe space. Additionally, I am an Intuitive Artist and use that as a medium to facilitate healing. I infuse all my art with Reiki and Light Language, which I channel during creation and can be found at www.igotthewoo.com. Coming soon are the "I Got the Woo! ™" subscription boxes which will have supplies such as cards, candles, incense, and more for the individual who is looking for tools and support in embracing their "Inner Woo" and shining their light fully. You can find me on IG currently as @CelticHealerShandra which will change to @IGotTheWoo when my trademark goes live, or on Facebook @igotthewoo. I look forward to connecting with you and teaching you too how to embrace your "WOO" and shine your light. Love and Light.

ABOUT THE AUTHOR
SHANDRA NICOLE SHULTZ

Ever since she was a young girl Shandra has been connected to the magickal, mystical and fantastical. An old soul whose kindness and compassion were unmatched, it is no surprise that she grew into the healer and spiritual coach that she has. Shandra works with womxn who have found themselves burnt-out, run down and ragged. She guides them on the transformational journey to finding their inner "WOO" and teaches them how to live their best life.

After almost a decade of searching to find her "WOO" again, Shandra found herself on a similar journey to what she now traverses with her clients. During her nine years of sobriety, Shandra has studied several different schools of thought, trained in many modalities, and walked a path of healing and self-discovery. She now blends these trainings with her intuitive knowledge, her spirituality, and connection to Gaia to guide womxn on their journey of self-discovery.

Shandra is a Shamanic Reiki Master, Spiritual Midwife, Celtic High Priestess, Witch, Integrative Life Coach, Intuitive Artist, Creatrix, Artificer, Divine Mother, Member/Ally of the LGBTQ+ community, and Owner of Healings of Light and Love by Shandra. She is the Creatrix of the 'I Got The Woo!™' community" and lives a life of adventure with her Partner Bjorn and their animal-children Brigid and Freya. She is the proud mom to one amazing kiddo who has always been her why.

Website: www.igotthewoo.com
@igotthewoo

17

TAMMY GOEN
A SENSITIVE JOURNEY

"You're SO sensitive!" "You're such a worry-wart, Tammy." "It's not a big deal; why can't you let it go?" Such were the frequent reminders throughout my childhood that I wasn't ok. And I told myself often that no one would ever understand me, that there was something inherently wrong with me—I was different and would never fit in. Oh, how I wanted to fit in, to be just like everyone else, to not think so much, and just have fun. But that would have meant I'd have to enjoy doing what others did (that I didn't) and not worry so damn much about others' feelings and the repercussions of my actions. No problem, right? Mmm-hmm.

Why couldn't I just let stuff go, ignore things that annoyed me, not worry about stuff so much, and not concern myself with what others thought, especially about me? Why was I so different than everyone else? And how would I ever learn to overcome these deficits with no one to talk with who understood me?

Actually, I didn't understand how others could NOT be concerned about certain things, could ignore annoying sounds, could not feel so intensely about everything and let go of feeling slighted by others. Sometimes it was easier to say nothing and just remain under the radar. Then I didn't need to hear about how wrong or odd I was. It was challenging to feel seen as different, so sometimes I opted for invisibility. At times being invisible was easier than having to explain my reactions, to be the only one to stand up for someone against rude comments, to be seen going against the norm, the expected. Being invisible meant being safer, but it was far from warm and fuzzy.

And energy—wow, could that be intense sometimes. I could feel when others were having an off day, or I could enter a room and feel the tension. A very memorable moment that occurred at age 15, began while chatting with both of my grandmothers and my mom in the family room. I decided to go listen to music in my room and said good-bye for now and headed down the hall. The moment I stepped through the doorway was like entering a vortex. I just stood there, taking in everything, wondering what had happened. Nothing seemed disturbed, and I couldn't identify what I was noticing, but something was off.

I scanned the room slowly, my eyes coming to rest at my stereo stand immediately to my right, and the handful of items displayed along both sides. I felt curious and wary, then ridiculous, and weird. I was quite fastidious and always kept things in their proper place, and I knew without question that two of the objects had changed places. Was this a problem? Certainly not. But how and why would they have been moved? Oddly, unlike in most families, my younger sister was never one to go into my room and bother my stuff, so I was sure that wasn't it. And they weren't broken or messy, just switched.

For a couple of long minutes, I stood there, trying to make sense of my discovery, trying to let it go—it wasn't important. But my curiosity would not be quelled; I had to figure it out. So, I headed slowly back down the hall, apprehensive but driven, to where my family still sat chatting. As soon as I entered, a hush came over the room. With an odd expression my mom asked, "What's up, Tam?" I hesitated, guarding my quirkiness for a moment longer, before revealing my dilemma. Rather than hearing that I must be imagining things, I cringed as laughter from all three of them filled the air. The joke was on me. My mother had been trying to explain just how sensitive and aware I was and said she could make the slightest change in my room, and I would know, and my grandmothers doubted her. Why would I notice such a small thing? Well, I proved her point. Although I felt no malice in any of these women—my role models and support system, it was another reminder of just how different I was.

Seeing my childhood through my now-knowing eyes, I feel immense gratitude for the love and support I received from my family. While I dealt with struggles in the social arena, in my childhood home I was seen as very (maybe even 'too') sensitive, yes, but I was accepted. My sensitivities may have been regarded as Tammy-quirks, but I wasn't judged negatively. This acceptance and support, which may not have always felt so, and only much later could I acknowledge the impact of it, helped me greatly as I navigated the world outside of my family. At home, I still felt misunderstood sometimes, but not wrong. In school and social activities, I was a square peg with sharp edges in a very smooth, round hole.

Being intellectual and a very good student gave meaning to my life, but it separated me that much more from the majority of my classmates. Thankfully, I did have the camaraderie of the handful of those who shared my focus on learning. I loved school itself, in spite of the social environment, and my coursework helped me gain more meaning out of such a challenging part of childhood. I just loved learning—it was easy for me to be fascinated by things and I wanted to understand it all. Curiosity may have killed the cat, but it served me well, most of the time.

While forever curious, I was also always creative and had a great affinity for everything artful and beautiful. I can't count the number of hours I spent creating: Lincoln Logs, Tinker Toys, Spirograph, Light Bright (with the make-your-own blank sheets), Doodle Art posters and countless coloring books, charcoal pencils and paper filled my non-study time. I navigated my social unease throughout middle and high school by focusing not only on my main studies, but with every art class I could fit into my schedule.

Art aligned well with my sensitivities and as I headed off to college, I was energized by my first steps toward an artistic career. A few weeks into my courses, however, an unrecognized desire to help others avoid unnecessary struggle won out over my well-laid plan for an art degree. As I sat in my first psychology course—simply an option I'd chosen to fill a gap in my schedule, tumblers in my heart fell into place and unlocked a previously unknown space. This was what I was supposed to do with my life—help others sort out their feelings, about life and about themselves. Although I didn't recognize it at the time, the goal of helping others offered a path toward softening all of the unease and discomfort I experienced throughout my childhood. And so began my journey toward a counseling career, the first step in a lifelong pursuit of guidance and healing of others and, as it turned out, of myself.

It was fulfilling and rewarding to help many others to reframe their difficulties, gain new understandings and let go of limiting beliefs holding them hostage. However, after thirteen years of helping clients, primarily survivors of trauma—child sexual abuse, physical abuse and domestic violence, I found myself face to face with intense burnout. And I'd lost my passion. I adjusted my case load and made various changes, but I had to acknowledge that I just couldn't do the work anymore. My burnout would make sense later, but at the time I felt frustrated and guilty for not being able to continue helping these clients. It was a struggle to let go of that for which I'd worked so hard, and to which I'd committed myself, and I so wanted to help, but it was time to move on.

So, I followed my heart and found myself again in school, this time for massage therapy and energy work. I needed to allow my emotional self to heal after such intense work and helping through the physical and energetic realm seemed a good fit. This new focus, especially the energy work, fed my curiosity and my desire to help, but after a number of years I once again found myself longing to be helping on an emotional level. I came full circle to coaching, incorporating all my education and experience to date, with more to come.

Yet, I still didn't truly understand myself. Oh, I'd done my personal work. I moved along in my self-growth journey through countless books, shamanic journeys, personal and group retreats, introspective exercises, and right-brain art projects, all bringing me one step closer to knowing myself and letting go of what didn't serve me. I valued these experiences greatly, and those who helped to guide me along the way. Still, full self-awareness eluded me. The golden nugget of understanding was just out of reach.

The individual stories of my challenges and blockages could fill this book, but they culminated on one memorable night ten years ago, at the age of forty-five. I'd agreed to join a couple of friends at a pre-event dinner with many people I didn't know and as I slid into the only seat available, I felt nearly invisible as my friends continued their conversations, giving me the very slightest acknowledgment. I was completely ignored by my friends for the duration of the dinner, wondering why they had bothered to invite me at all. My food mostly eaten, though hardly enjoyed, I left the party, receiving the coolest of good-byes from both. My confusion was immense, the pain deep in my heart and gut. Over the following two weeks I attempted to address the issue with my friends, never feeling understood, but instead I heard, again, "It's not a big deal. Just let it go."

Then it happened—the moment that would change my life, thankfully, for the better. A friend who listened attentively to my woes lovingly recommended searching online for traits of Highly Sensitive People, and I found a self-test. To say that finding and taking this inventory was powerful is like saying Niagara Falls is a pretty little waterfall. Here in print was a list of all the things I felt, the way I saw the world, how I thought, as if someone had accessed an inner vault of my being-ness and given it a new language. I felt more validation for who I was from those 16 sentences than from all of my personal work until that moment.

I was a Highly Sensitive Person (HSP). Obviously, I'd always known I was sensitive (as in TOO sensitive), but this was a new way of understanding it. I wasn't weird, unreasonable, ridiculous, wrong, needing to be fixed, nor—and this was the most significant—alone. There were obviously others; someone created an inventory and shared it on the internet!

Thus began my mission to learn all I could about High Sensitivity. I discovered that there were not just a few others like me, but potentially up to 20% of the population experiencing life in a similar way. That in itself was nearly unimaginable. Suddenly I was part of a whole tribe I hadn't even been aware existed. And bonus—it's an inherent trait. I hadn't created or made up my experience for some kind of secondary gain. It was real. And in that moment, as I contemplated the 14 out of 16 characteristics I'd checked off on the inventory, I saw my whole life—past and present, through a shiny new crystal lens of clarity. I was a lot of things, those I liked and those I wanted to change, but under it all, I was just Highly Sensitive.

Learning that there was a reason for my sensitivity, my challenges of letting things go, feeling so deeply, having such a hard time dealing with others' behaviors and the injustices of the world, created an oceanic wave of compassion for myself, for my little girl who had struggled while trying to make sense of a crazy world and for my adult self who thought she should have figured herself out, figured life out, by now. I was Highly Sensitive—I was in the minority, but I was OK.

You may be reading and thinking, "Wow, this sounds so much like me!" or someone you know. But what is High Sensitivity exactly? And why can't we just choose to not be so sensitive?

First, it's important to identify what High Sensitivity is NOT: a diagnosis, a disorder, a condition that needs to be fixed or something to "get over." It's also not introversion (30% of HSPs are extroverted) or shyness. High Sensitivity, or Sensory Processing Sensitivity, is a trait, like left handedness, that's all about processing information. Elaine Aron, the psychologist and primary researcher who coined the term, describes it using the acronym DOES:

~Depth of Processing. We process all information deeply and thoroughly. Everything is important, even things that others haven't even noticed or were able to let go of easily and quickly. We may process things for days! Have you ever told someone you needed to think about something, then get back with them a few days later and they don't even remember what you're talking about? Mmm-hmm.

~Overstimulation/Overwhelm: HSPs are like sponges, with fewer or less effective filters. It can be difficult to ignore things, to handle competing sounds and activity around us, to cope with the energy of many people. We can become completely exhausted from these things and retreat, become ill or blow up. If my nervous system is calm and I'm prepared, I can enjoy myself at an outdoor festival for an hour or so, if the music isn't too loud and there's a lot of space. A crowded, noisy indoor venue—not going to happen.

~Emotionality: We feel our emotions intensely and can be challenged in expressing them appropriately. We often need to avoid news, media and many types of movies, because they're just too painful—the sadness, fear, disappointment, disrespect, inhumane treatment. It's just too much to handle. When I saw the movie Amistad, I bawled about it for a week and felt like I had PTSD. I haven't watched similar movies since.

~Sensing the Subtle: HSPs notice every little thing most of the time. We're the canaries in the coal mine, aware of things others miss. We notice when things aren't quite right, we're good at finding things because we recognize very subtle differences in our surroundings. I actually prevented my house from likely burning down one night when I awoke from a deep sleep smelling something burning. Once I was awake, I discovered that the hot electrical odor was so faint I was only able to locate it while searching my living room on my hands and knees, yet it woke me in the next room. Eventually I discovered that the wires of a baseboard heater had become one hot, melted mass.

Becoming aware of myself through my new lens of sensitivity, reframing my entire life to that point, was like re-reading an old book I thought I knew by heart and realizing I'd missed an entire chapter every time. It changed not only the meaning of the whole story but created an entirely new ending. With clarity and understanding, so much potential was uncovered and realized.

I began to relish each moment of clarity and validation, and to develop a deeper sense of self love and send it out to the universe. And my circle of friends began to shift. It had always seemed like proof of my strangeness that I had a very small group of friends and had little interest in spending my time in large groups of people I didn't know or with those I knew as acquaintances, but really knew nothing about. And to be honest, I didn't care to know more. I was content with my good friends, and with my time alone. And in fact, I had a very rich inner world, with unceasing imagination and a desire to learn, learn, learn. I never could understand how anyone could be bored. But I had always deemed this all to be undesirable or at least proof that I wasn't normal.

Learning about High Sensitivity, and that this is normal in the HSP world, I was able to release my self-judgment and social expectations and just enjoy time with myself and my small group of friends. Then I began to attract more Highly Sensitives into my inner circle, and what a relief to feel understood and accepted just for who I am. The majority of my friends now are HSP, and it makes such a difference. I also came to learn how to put into perspective the responses and behaviors of my non-Highly Sensitive friends, to see how they originate through a different lens and not experience them as disrespectful or uncaring.

Highly Sensitives have a very different way of experiencing the world than non-HSPs; we're just wired differently. Not superior, not inferior, not good, not bad; it's just the way it is. And you may be hesitant to get stuck with a label or think maybe it would just be used as a crutch, an excuse for what's not working. I was concerned about this as well—I longed to feel special for who I am, but not at risk of seeming arrogant or portraying superiority. It's not something to absolve us from responsibilities, either, nor allow us to receive special treatment, and it's definitely not an excuse. It IS a way to understand ourselves and our experience of life, and to help others do the same. And if we can embrace our sensitivities, they can become our Super Power.

I soon was recognizing just how amazing my sensitivities were, and could be, if I stopped discounting or trying to avoid or hide them. How blessed I am to be able to notice, and relish, the littlest things in life—a ladybug on a new spring leaf that others didn't notice, the distant melody of coyote songs out of others' range of hearing or awareness. My curiosity and desire to know all sides of something, to process situations until I've solved the problem completely, are deeply satisfying. Heightened intuition helps me on a personal level and while working with clients. And I celebrate my creative, artistic side. While compassion and empathy can lead to pain and sadness, they can also provide very rich connection and a sharing of immense joy. Life is in technicolor, and I would choose that over black and white any day.

It's important that we HSPs remind ourselves of the positive characteristics of our trait when we start to feel the weight of the world. It's also important to take care of ourselves. Throughout my Sensitive journey, I've been so grateful for my healthy self-care practices. HSPs require a boost in this area in order to cope with the world with minimal overwhelm. We soak up life like sponges with less effective filters and our nervous systems get overloaded much more easily. Life is amazing, but we lose sight of that easily if we're in a constant state of fight or flight. A daily practice of meditation or mindfulness techniques, alone time, healthy lifestyle and good sleep are imperative. I'm adding frequently to my self-care regimen and love to share my techniques with others.

As I began the coaching direction of my helping career, I used my sensitivities to understand my clients' struggles, to "get" what they were feeling and discover a sense of what would help them. This had been the case while I worked as a counselor, of course, but now I was aware of how I was able to do this. Then came an intriguing, though not surprising, awareness: the majority of my clients were also Highly Sensitive. Like attracted like and HSPs were finding me, even when they didn't yet know they were Highly Sensitive. I think there aren't many things as powerful as being understood. I've heard from clients that previous counseling and coaching seemed to only take them so far, and that they never felt like they were truly accepted and understood. Highly Sensitives being understood completely by an HSP coach or counselor is priceless. Realizing that this niche was underserved led to my focus on helping Highly Sensitive souls on their journeys.

Becoming aware of and embracing the High Sensitivity trait allows for the blooming of our full potential. Being HSP isn't all about struggle; it's also about allowing the vibrant tapestry of life to flow forth. By learning to value and celebrate our sensitive characteristics, instead of hiding, minimizing or feeling embarrassed by them, we can turn them into our Super Power. More than ever before, the world needs our empathy and compassion, our ability to think out of the box and see all sides, our creativity and dedication. It's time for Sensitive Souls to shine our light, to be seen, heard and understood, and celebrated for the strengths with which our sensitivities endow us. It's time for Highly Sensitive People to be recognized as Highly Sensational People.

ABOUT THE AUTHOR
TAMMY GOEN

Tammy is a self-love and happiness coach for Highly Sensitive People. As an HSP she knows first-hand what it's like to feel misunderstood, unaccepted, overwhelmed and needing to be fixed.

She's felt the self-loathing and shame and struggled in relationships and felt totally incapable of dealing with the atrocities of life and in spite of it all she learned how to thrive... how to love herself and embrace and enjoy her sensitivities and all that life has to offer.

Tammy helps other Highly Sensitive People to reframe their pasts, let go of old beliefs and patterns that keep them stuck and develop coping strategies and a deep sense of self-acceptance and self-love. Using her degree in Counselling Psychology, her certifications in EFT/Tapping and HeartMath meditation and other meditation and mindfulness practices and energy healing techniques, she guides HSPs toward realizing their Superpower.

She loves witnessing their "Aha!" moments as they gain new self-awareness and understanding and embrace their sensitive journeys.

linktr.ee/tammygoen

18

TE ARAHI "THE GUIDE" & KATI LUDWIG

THE WEAVING OF ANCESTRAL WISDOM

PART 1 - THE ETHNIC WARRIOR BY TE ARAHI

*K*ohu woke with a start. As her eyes adjusted to the light, it confirmed this wasn't a dream, and her father had indeed returned home. She rose from her pikau mattress on the dirt floor and peered around the side of the thatched wall that supported the whare (house) from where she could hear voices. "Yes, it's true," she heard her father say, "my brother is dead. He was captured, tortured, and killed by the Ngati Whatua near Pouto". As she strained her neck further, she glimpsed his head drop as he ushered the words. Finally, she understood that the rumours that had been floating through the village the last few days were true—her uncle Kiwiroa was dead.

It had been said that Kiwiroa had unknowingly entered a sacred area there, a place where several children from the tribe of Ngati Whatua had died in a landslide last winter. Since this sad event, a rahui (restriction) of entry had been put on that place. Now that cursed piece of land had claimed another victim, Kiwiroa, a warrior of Ngati Manu and the younger brother of Te Whareumu, the senior leader of their tribe at Kororareka.

As his words hung in the air Kohu dropped her head; knowing the brutality her father was renowned for on the battlefield, he would soon be turning the deep loss of his brother into an aggressive assault on those who had lured him to his death. On her hands and knees, Kohu crept forward, and as she drew closer, she saw her mother Moehuri embracing the lithe muscle-bound titan as he sagged into his wife's shoulder. Kohu sensed the sadness with which her father had spoken these words. For all his renown and fame as a brutal warrior, she knew only too well the loving father and brother he was. Behind the closed thatched doors, Te Whareumu quietly grieved for his brother while being comforted in a loving embrace by his wife, Moehuri. The moments lingered on as he rested his head on her shoulder, and she held him close to her. Eventually, he lifted his head and retreated to sit down on the thatch bedding that covered the floor. He stared off into the distance as he gathered his thoughts. Kohu could see that the moment of grieving in loving silence had passed, and she knew her father well enough to know that what he was doing now was planning, and she instinctively knew what he was planning for—revenge!

Kohu turned away, retreating into her thoughts. Her uncle Kiwiroa had been a calm man, making his mark as a fisherman and hunter of repute for their people. It had been a trading venture that had taken him away from their east coast village and crossed over to the western coastline of Northland known as (te tai tama tane)—the boy's side. This coastal strip was named so because of its rugged and weathered coastline. While there, Kiwiroa had been befriended by a small group of the Ngati Whatua tribesman who had given him lodgings and treated him with the hospitality required to a man of his status. Later they deliberately led him into the forbidden area knowing full well that his fate would be death once he was discovered to have broken this restriction by entering onto the land.

The foreboding of imminent bloodshed hung in the air with a heavy presence. This was not the end but the beginning between Ngati Manu and Ngati Whatua. And, although as a young girl child she could not understand why Ngati Whatua would want her uncle killed, looking at her father now though, she knew that death awaited many at the hands of Ngati Manu and their allies through the leadership of Te Whareumu.

Te Whareumu returned from his thoughts and let his eyes fall gently on to his young daughter peering from around the corner. Now aware that she had been seen, Kohu tried to duck away back into bed. "Taihoa!" her father called out, "Haere mai e ko, hoki mai ki taku awhi." Hearing this, she stopped her retreat and made her way back into the main room of the small hut and ran, falling into his powerful arms. She could smell the dry sweat on his skin, and she knew he had been running most of the past three days to arrive back at their kainga (home). Dawn was only a few short hours away, and with it would come the planning and preparation for the revenge of her uncles' life.

For now, though, she enjoyed the moment wrapped in her father's arms as he drew her close to him, and they shared the pain of loss of their families' uncle and brother.

MY ANCESTOR TE WHAREUMU – THE LEADER, PEACEMAKER, AND ECONOMIST

The writing above is an excerpt taken from a book written on the life of Maori leader Te Whareumu. The central character of the book is Kohu, my great-great-grandmother, and the book is based on letters passed down over the generations within our family. The death of Kiwiroa was a factual event that took place in 1818 – and is reported to have led to the battle of *te ika a ranginui*, a huge battle that changed the power structure of the northern Maori tribes of New Zealand at the time.

Undoubtedly, Te Whareumu was a warrior of note, and in 1820 rose to become the leader of his people in the Bay of Islands in New Zealand. This was a huge period of development in New Zealand's history, and at the time Te Whareumu rose to power Kororareka (or Russell to use its English name) was the **economic powerhouse of the country** due to the steady arrival of the global whaling fleet in kororareka to rest and restock as the sailors pursued their prey—the giant blue whales—into the southern ocean.

This meant my ancestor had to navigate an extremely delicate and potentially dangerous situation as the sailors interacted with the local Maori. They were known globally as *the hellhole of the pacific* because of the sailors' needs for fresh food, timber, alcohol, and women. It fell to Te Whareumu as the local chief to ensure the well-being of his people was met as these 'foreigners' brought economic prosperity to Kororareka—indeed, returning to the factual death of Kiwiroa in the story earlier. His death happened only because he had gone to Ngati Whatua territory to gather wild pigs to supply the whaling ships anchored in the harbour of his home village.

Also, during Te Whareumus's reign, he had to navigate his tribe through the 'power shift' in the Bay of Islands as this new race (called 'Pakeha' by the Maori) arrived with their superior technology on the shores of Aotearoa – New Zealand.

In short, when Te Whareumu was born, Pakeha couldn't survive in Aotearoa without Maori protection and food. By the time of his death in 1822, Maori were well on their way to becoming 'second class citizens' in their own country (as unfortunately is the case with most global indigenous peoples) – and something that we, as Maori, are still battling to overcome today in 2021. [see graph below] [1]

https://www.stats.govt.nz	Non-Maori	Maori
Average life expectancy in years	Male 81 Female 84	Male 73 Female 77
Own their own home	56.8%	28.2%
Prison percentages	30%	52%
Unemployment percentages	6%	12.9%

Leadership styles fascinate me, and I often wonder what it must have been like for Te Whareumu as my ancestor dealt with the social landscape of the time. They had to deal with the huge problems that inevitably arose by the interactions between not only two races of people, but also the values that these very different groups had, and of course, the power structures that were in play as New Zealand transitioned from global discovery to becoming a colony of the British empire. This must have been incredibly difficult for him.

TE ARAHI ELLIS BRYERS - ME

Born by my Pakeha mum, who had red hair and blue eyes, and my Maori dad, I grew up in an era in New Zealand, i.e., the 1970s-80s, where as a child I was told "learning things Maori isn't important anymore—we live in a Pakeha world now, you need to become a builder or something like that," and so understandably I learnt nothing about my Maori ancestry – it wasn't until I was 27 years of age that I spoke my first words of *te reo Maori* (the Maori language). By now, it was 1993, and the social attitude towards 'honouring Maori knowledge and practices' had changed considerably. Therefore I entered the 'greenstone door' of empowerment.... and I never looked back.

Presently my vocation is as an 'educator' where I design and deliver a government-funded community youth programme targeting youth between 12-18 years of age. To qualify for the programme, the participants have to be *youth offenders or siblings of youth offenders*. I am tasked to engage with 50 young people a year, and **of the 150 young men I have engaged with in the past three years, 147 of them have been Maori.**

Coming back to the title of this book, *"Evolving on purpose; Mindful ancestors paving the way for future generations'*, every day, I go to work with the mission of changing the statistics in the graph above. I say to the boys, "Our ancestors never meant for us to be disempowered in our own country—they want us to live enriched, comfortable and happy lives." Of course, we then go on a journey of empowerment through the six weeks they are with me on the programme to learn and embed practices and tools that allow them to access the pathway to living exactly that in the future.

MY CHILDREN

Following on down the ancestral line to my son and my daughter, the twists of *evolving of purpose* continues. Like me, when they were children, they *didn't learn te reo Maori. However,* they have grown up with the confidence to believe in themselves and their abilities. They have the resilience to meet challenges and overcome adversity, and as young adults, I see them as living empowered lives.

As a parent, for me, that is enough. I am grateful to see my children living well and with the resilience to meet challenges while showing love, wisdom, respect, and care for people. They have both come to know that finding your passion—a passion which excites you and calls you to take action—and by surrounding that passion with your skills and talents, then given momentum displayed by committing time and effort to it. This brings reward.

These are the ethics that I endeavour to influence into the young men that I 'hang out' with so that they have some keys to unlock and experience a life well-lived.

PART 2 - A JOURNEY INTO EMBODIED FEMININE WISDOM BY KATI LUDWIG

I find myself in an ancient, magical forest. The sun is shining pleasantly through the roof of the forest, but there are also dark, cold corners. The air is filled with secrets, mysteries, and wisdom; some unravelled before and some yet to be discovered. A mystical woman appears out of the thicket of the forest. She is the guardian of the forest; an Earth Goddess radiating natural beauty, compassion, kindness, and deep inner knowing from the depth of her being. I know I am encountering the powerful feminine presence of the Earth Mother who has come to remind me of my essence and strength in her loving, gentle way. Her kind gaze and infinite loving energy softly invite me to enter a dark looking, cold cave. As I walk through the narrow entrance of the cave, I feel a warm glow in my heart and a voice whispering, "You carry the essence within you. Trust in the journey". As I walk deeper into the cave, it opens up, and a giant, pulsating heart filled with red-golden light appears. The deep, pulsating sound fills me with peace and trust. I am arriving home. Something from within tells me I am in the centre of my feminine essence: my inner capacity for limitless healing, powerful transformation, and unconditional love. I am being offered the red-golden light of transformation in exchange for my inner dark cloud – the cloud of holding on to control, having to know it all, judgments, and limitations. As I humbly surrender my blockages and limitations to the heart of red-golden light, the dark cloud turns into red-golden light too. And it is in this moment that I deeply remember my innate capacity to transform and renew. I leave the cave in deep gratitude, and as I step out of the cave into the forest, my paternal grandfather appears. His eyes are filled with love and peace as he is looking at me. A painful question bubbles up inside of me: "Why did you not see me as the little girl I was?" and I feel resistance to connect with him and let him close to me. And there is this voice inside of me again whispering softly, "You know the truth. You carry the essence within you." and in this moment, I feel a dark cloud of blame and judgment leaving my body from the centre of my chest through my throat and mouth into the sky. And I can see my grandfather in his true essence; I can see his love and in his wounding. I feel my heart being filled with the red-golden glow radiating the medicine of forgiveness and freedom. Feeling liberated from my past, from judgments, and from social conditioning. Feeling free to be the woman I was always meant to be. Feeling connected to the resources, strengths, and wisdom of my ancestors. And I remember this is the journey.

Being birthed into this world gifted with a free spirit, gentle soul, and strong will, I have been confronted with a myriad of challenges to overcome and invitations to grow and expand. I was born in former communist East Germany, being lovingly cared for by parents who have been raised by parents carrying the scars and wounds of war. My paternal grandfather returned from war with only one arm, and his heart filled with anger and piled up unresolved trauma. I remember feeling scared of him as a little girl. His inner terror and helplessness to deal with his trauma caused him to reject himself— and consequently, aggressively rejecting the people around him, including my grandmother, my father, and myself. Growing up in an oppressive system where a healthy, embodied engagement with the so called "Schuldfrage" (guilt question) was not encouraged and where family, friends, and neighbours were set up against each other to guarantee system conformation through the "STASI" (Ministry for State Security) was challenging. There was the energy of confusion, uncertainty, guilt, taboo subjects, suppression of feelings, and inhibition of life's full expression. And there was love, hope, resilience, resourcefulness, joy, and laughter too. I remember feeling confused about who and how I was meant to be as a girl/woman, and there were many unspoken expectations floating around in between the lines. I remember once, as a girl, when I allowed myself to express my true nature with volume and assertiveness, my grandmother said to me a girl had to be good and demure. As a young girl, I was not encouraged to discover and develop my spiritual connection simply because spirituality and higher wisdom were rendered as taboo subjects not worthwhile exploring further. With the Berlin wall coming down and the promise of freedom arising in people's hearts, my journey of breaking out of conventional norms and limitations started gaining momentum. I began studying psychology, and I discovered my passion for travelling. I felt incredibly inspired by delving into different cultures, getting to experience different ways of being and living, and acquiring different perspectives on reality. Each outer journey was also an inner journey of expansion. I started feeling my connection to spirit, and with that, my trust to listen to my inner intuitive voice grew. This voice guided me into exploring and integrating ancient healing modalities into my psychology practice. I realized my journey of becoming an empowered healer in service of the feminine wisdom had begun. And so did my journey of confronting and overcoming doubts, fears, and limitations: "Do I know enough to be a healer?"; "Is what I have to offer valuable?"; "Can I trust in myself?" I had been spending years acquiring qualifications and certificates to be a 'healer', yet inside I had doubts whether I really could be helpful, useful, and of value to others. I had been rejecting my feminine intuition and wisdom for a long time. I simply did not realize that embracing my feminine intuition and wisdom was not only enough but THE magical ingredient for being of service to others. Little had I known this was the beginning of various rites of passage into learning about my feminine needs, boundaries, and being seen as the woman I am. It was my journey into authentic self-care. Learning how to be continually receptive, soft, neutral, and empathic whilst acknowledging and honouring my feminine needs and nature has been invaluable in my personal practice and to the people, I work with.

My story is one example of manifestation by stepping into the full expression of womanhood and the mysteries of the feminine – season by season, step by step, and breath by breath in our own unique rhythm. It is a deep remembering of encapsulated wisdom in our hearts, bones, and souls. Just like Joanne L. Shenandoah sings in her song "Path of Beauty":

I will walk the path of beauty
Light forever shining
Healing power of love flow through me
To the hearts of humankind
It is time to live in peace
Mind and hearts wide open
Piercing through the veil of darkness
To the light of heaven

Time to lay aside the judgment
Of each other's duty
In the walk that we must make
May we find the path of beauty
We must learn to live in peace
Selfless love's compassion
Looking only for the goodness
In each other's actions

I am walking this path of beauty, I am opening my heart, and I am allowing myself to trust and shine. Through the power of forgiveness and by seeking and seeing the truth, I build and strengthen my connection to the resources and wisdom of my ancestral field. I am a woman.

PART 3 - THE WEAVING: JOINT WISDOM OF OUR STORIES

As we evolve, we draw from the positive and negative teachings of our ancestors. Only we can decipher what is beneficial for our reality in the here and now, which of course, is different from our ancestor's reality. The path of mindful evolution can be the key to the process of un-conditioning ourselves from trauma passed on from our ancestors and leads us to the integration of valuable resources, values, and strengths. The inner journey is both and requires embodying the energies of love, acceptance—as opposed to judgment, humility, and forgiveness.

As Te Arahi states, his story is about reclaiming the inner sovereignty that was taken from his ancestors through the process of colonization. In his view, it is a noble quest to overcome this process by honouring our ancestors' wishes and being empowered to live lives of fulfilment in 2021 and beyond. While it is clear he feels we have an obligation to our ancestors, we also know that when demands are placed upon us, as outlined by Kati's story, these obligations can become burdens that need to be overcome. It is important to remember we all are doing the best we can at any given moment in any given situation and that despite life's challenges and demands, it is a beautiful world we live in filled with the possibility to love ourselves and those around us. And most importantly, to have fun while we are here!

And so the journey goes on...

---

1. https://www.stats.govt.nz

ABOUT THE AUTHOR
TE ARAHI "THE GUIDE"

Te Arahi is a modern day guide who assists individuals to uncover ancient wisdoms.

By supporting them in utilizing these practices they are empowered to overcome adversity and develop resilience to move forward and live the life of their dreams.

Steeped in the indigenous Maori knowledge and practices of his ancestors,

Te Arahi brings heart and love to his various vocations and a light soul to his life's journey.

TED Talk:
www.youtube.com/watch?v=J9uEiA9YTXM&t=688s
Facebook business page:
www.facebook.com/taiaha.nz
Website: www.TeArahi.com

ABOUT THE AUTHOR
KATI LUDWIG

Kati Ludwig, A hybrid-healer who weaves spirit and energy medicine through her scientific background of clinical psychology. She transforms her client's lives to be hopeful, stable and empowered.

You are your own guru. Be inspired by your own story.

Your answers lie within you, you only need the tools to access them.

Kati's mission is to help people to hold space for themselves and to achieve steadfast inner peace. She approaches the biology and the hardened industry of clinical dis-ease with a maternal, soulful presence. Kati has mastered traditional cognitive therapy, but her piercing eyes and understanding reach into one's body, far surpassing the limits of the mind, in order to meet the soul exactly where it is and coax it back into its full vitality.

Further information on Kati: www.kati-ludwig.com

19

TRACEY KISSOON
I HAVE ALWAYS WONDERED WHY THERE IS SUCH A DISTINCTION BETWEEN SCIENCE AND SPIRITUALITY

*a*s I sit down to write this chapter, evolving on purpose, I realised that maybe 50% of the time I have done so consciously and the other 50%, of life and its ever-changing nature has placed the issue forcefully in front of me, so that I could not take another step without dealing with the pile of manure in front of me. Sometimes avoiding the issue has taken me on such wonderful, interesting adventures; so of course, I did not want to deal with any issues, as I was too busy enjoying the adventure and freedom.

All of us experience loss, grief, change in various forms; but it is what, if anything, we are willing to do with those chapters that makes the difference. In some areas, I feel like a baby just learning to take small steps and, in others, a weary veteran. It is all learning and enriching. Do I regret some things I have done? Yes I do. Do I regret the lessons I learnt? No. I feel fortunate that I have asked the questions and attempted to evolve consciously. Every day I realise that my external circumstances reflect what I have consciously and unconsciously created for myself. On the outside, I live in the wonderful Cotswolds. I have work that I love, I have a supportive and good husband, and we have two lovely healthy daughters. There are challenges and dysfunctional patterns within every area that I would like to improve. I am working on it, and I am learning (never too late at 55) that the changes happen on the inside first.

A bit of background. I am the first generation of immigrant parents, both from former British colonies. My grandparents on my mother's side escaped from Burma and the communist regime in the late 1950s. My father came from the West Indies to England to study medicine but never did. I was born in Clapham/London in August 1966, some 10 weeks early and less than 2lb in weight. I was not expected to survive as special care baby units had not yet been invented. My childhood was confusing and difficult, and although I was very capable and responsible, the emotional baggage that it left me with, I am still dealing with. They are both a blessing and a curse.

When I was nine years old, I looked around me and realised very clearly that we were all imprisoned in some way. Those around me (adults) had so little ambition and expectation for themselves, and in turn me. That day, I made a very deliberate and conscious decision to become as educated as I could and leave this ghetto. There were two things I wanted to achieve; have a profession and travel. My mother thought differently. In her opinion I should get these "fancy ideas out of my head" as what I wanted and what I got in life would be two different things. Her ambitions for me were, to learn to type, work in a typing pool, leave school at 16, marry and have children. Since I would never be the breadwinner, my education wasn't deemed in any way important. It wasn't just the fact that we had very little, (I had my precious books, siblings and a park to play in), it was the constant belittling, beating, and blurring of boundaries that made life, at times, feel intolerable.

I was accepted at St. Mary's Hospital, Paddington in London, to train as a Physiotherapist in 1983, I made it! My first ambition was on the way to being achieved. The way Physiotherapy was organised then was to have lectures in the hospital and University and to have practicals in the second year. In total, that meant we were reasonably prepared for treating real patients. During clinical placement I often got into trouble for the way I handled things. I was not negligent or inappropriate. On reflection, I think I just reasoned in a different way; I followed energy and noticed small details about patients that made them unique. It struck me very early on how different people responded to being in hospital. I was drawn to the sad and lonely as I felt they needed more compassion, understanding, and support. It was an instinctual response and definitely not encouraged, as it was not scientific! Those who had family and lots of support, especially after heart surgery, did so much better. To me, it was such an honour to have a patient's trust that, in some small way, I felt I needed to earn it more. I asked deeper questions; I wanted to know about them, what mattered to them, what inspired them. Mostly this was met with enthusiasm and a willingness to share these things, other times confusion about how this was relevant to the issue at hand. The words of my tutors I took very seriously. It was my job to work out the patient's motivations and inspire them to comply with advice for their own wellbeing. I interpreted this more like a collaboration between myself and my patient. We needed each other, and perhaps I could lead some aspects of the relationship. I loved working on the wards. I worked with the nurses and other health professionals so that the patients had a good experience. If someone needed to use the bathroom, I would take them. Not only did it give them confidence after surgery but independence too. I have never understood therapists who waited for the nurse to get the bedpan, commode, or whatever. If you need to go, you can't wait hours for a nurse to be free. Possibly for no other reason than this, my philosophy was a success!

Then came my second ambition. After college I had a serious case of wanderlust. I taught English in Cairo, worked on a Kibbutz and travelled around East Africa with the Swedish love of my life.

Next stop was South East Asia with a year's visa to work in Australia. What actually happened is we both fell in love with Indonesia and this became our home for the next four years. Two of them were in Bali - what a jewel. A very different feel as this island is Hindu. Everywhere can be seen temples, offerings, and celebrations of the Hindu calendar. This wondrous place gave me an education of an entirely different kind. The way the Balinese weave and integrate their spiritual lives into daily life is spectacular and a wondrous sight to behold. Here I learnt about the tangible but invisible matrix of energy available to us. I now believe this is our electric field that has been there all along; perhaps science just wasn't able or willing to admit it. I observed and learned the spiritual practices of meditation, good eating, and self-love. These all help to build a strong foundation of physical, emotional and spiritual health. Meditation and yoga all help to calm the chatty critical brain and alter the workings of the Central Nervous System. By that I mean, in Western Society, the way we live overloads our senses and nervous system to the point where our brains and bodies are screaming. This alters all of the electrical communication systems and is one of the roots of chronic diseases, and possibly the mental health crisis we face today. I now understand this in a different light; we can change our electrical field, make it stronger or weaker by our actions. Our electrical field is our defence, strength, and depending on what signals we emit, we attract. This is science yet is also spirituality and vice versa. This may well be a key to healing chronic diseases. I truly believe the answers to some of the dilemmas we are facing are actually staring us in the face.

In Bali itself, I saw and experienced electrical fields and healing directly; I sustained a terrible ligament tear on my ankle; I had been invited onto a boat sailing towards Lombok, and I was so looking forward to it. The first evening I dived off the end of the boat and managed to twist my left ankle badly while doing so—ouch. It swelled up like a balloon, throbbed like hell, I could not walk on it, and was incredibly painful. Still, I enjoyed my time on the boat and splashed about in the sea. When we hit land, one of the crew suggested I see a healer. I went off to see him. As it turned out he and

I worked at the same complex, where I was setting up the lab for vanilla testing.

I could hardly believe my eyes, this healer held my foot which by this time was like wearing a cement boot, then removed his hands and focused on them about 25 cm/12 inches away, and I could feel something—energy, a force—and my ankle in front of my eyes started to go down. Within ten minutes or less, it looked like the right one. I was amazed and delighted, paid him the equivalent of £2, and literally skipped off. This is commonplace in Bali, the first port of call for many is to see a healer or Dukon before a doctor. Unfortunately, energy healing can be used both ways, and this is also prevalent in Bali too.

After two amazing years on this wonderful island, life imploded for me. My business failed, I was seriously unwell, and the love of my life and I parted ways. When I returned to England, I felt like I had landed on a different planet. At this point, I spoke fluent Bahasa and dreamt in Indonesian. I returned to my profession in the NHS, but things had changed so much, not always in the best way either! Attitudes towards patients had changed. Everything had to be documented in triplicate. There were so many rules and regulations that were impossible to follow, which meant they were frequently broken. I felt like a fish out of water. I could not relate to my colleagues, and they could not relate to me! It was a lonely time. However, due to horrible staff shortages and senior staff either part-time or off on long-term sickness, I took charge of several new grads and locums in a busy West London hospital. I loved mentoring and supporting them. It uplifted me seeing them grow in ability and confidence.

I championed the patients that were written off by consultants and the medical profession in general. Here I cemented my belief that the human mind and body working together is a truly powerful force. I argued and won; a backward policy was changed. Quite early on after a stroke, the brain shuts down for at least 48 hours to protect itself (to me, this was obvious), but it is at the brain shut down phase that the Consultant and team often seem to deliver the prognosis to anxiously waiting relatives. Some people really shut down and are barely responsive. I thought this was horribly unfair because at least half of these people walk out and recover to live a full and active life. During the first week after a stroke, many patients cannot swallow or tolerate food. A naso-gastric tube is often used to give the patient calories. Unfortunately, because it is so invasive, many pull it out repeatedly as they are still in shut down or half unconscious. Many consultants and registrars keep reinserting it, wasting time and resources, and causing further distress. It is at this crucial point where a person needs calories to survive, yet are not getting them. The medical team did not seem to join the dots and would question why the patient was not progressing. I remember getting incredibly exasperated and explaining that if patients don't have enough calories, then they start to break down their own muscles to help with the calorie deficit. Thankfully now, these patients can be PEG fed, (Percutaneous endoscopic gastrostomy - a tube with liquid nutrition directly into the stomach) and go on to have this removed and often walk out with their relatives. So, I could champion patients and new graduates but not yet myself.

An incident with a 20 stone lady that landed on me, gave me further lessons. It both piqued my interest in Musculo-skeletal Physiotherapy and forced me to look after myself. My colleagues, much to my amazement, helped to patch me back together. This led me to decide to pursue this speciality with keen interest. I had never felt good enough or able enough to do this, but luckily some opportunities came my way, which enabled both to happen.

First, I moved to the Cotswolds. The second thing that was key was a charity called SOCA (Survivors of Child Abuse). Thanks to the beautiful countryside, and group therapy, I was able to let go of some of the hurt and shame, learnt that I could say no, and more. It was humbling to me that some of the most horrifically abused children, if they get help, become incredible adults. Compassion, love, and laughter were potent medicines for the body, mind and soul.

The opportunity to learn more about musculo-skeletal medicine came in the form of a double-ended sword. It was a steep and intense learning curve and I was horribly bullied. Having not really practiced this discipline much since I graduated, I was thrust into this monstrous machine with little preparation! I had some great colleagues, but there was also a new breed of Physiotherapist with different qualities. It was no longer enough to get good outcomes for patients, crunch the waiting list, mentor new staff, we had to prove our clinical reasoning, and everything had to be evidence-based. I welcomed this change as research was becoming more prevalent within the profession; it became a positive challenge. Some Trusts in Gloucestershire threw the baby out with the bathwater and became completely hands-off as early as 2000, which I believed to be counterproductive for everyone. Yet again Patients missed out the most!

I was almost always the object of ridicule since I often used Reflexology and Acupuncture with my patients to improve their healing rates, calm the overwrought nervous system, and a whole host of other valid reasons. Often I would be hauled into the head Physio's office wondering what I had done wrong this time! I would get shouted at for rubbing out in the diary, late paperwork, or some irrelevant detail. I remember a particular time after being shouted out for 10 straight minutes, I timidly asked if everything was okay with my clinical work. She paused for breath and said, "that's another thing—every week I get a phone call about you from patients, nurses GPs" (me thinks- oh shit), "they keep praising you and are delighted with their outcomes, and insist that only you treat their referrals," (me - okay so what is the problem?) "just remember you are the same as us, don't think you are anything special." Phew, I skipped out, relieved that really there was nothing wrong. It took me several years to shake off the idea that I was utterly useless at my profession. A chance conversation at a particular course, with another physio (who happened to work for Manchester City Football Club) was hugely pivotal in understanding what all of those experiences were about. He said "you do realise why they bullied you dont you?" not really, "it was, quite clearly about you showing them up, you were so much better, and so unaware of that." Wow, that had not really occurred to me.

In hindsight, I acknowledge I probably was not easy to manage. I put patients first, sometimes before myself, which frankly was a recipe for disaster at some point. Looking back, my manager was mirroring my mother's behaviour towards me, so whilst it stung, I was already used to it. I made coffee for my colleagues, helped them out if they were running behind, and did my best to make all our loads bearable. It came naturally to me; I wasn't trying, it was just the way I saw things. At the time I believed that I was only worth something if I was offering to others, not just for being me. My outer world and experiences kept reflecting that back, which only reinforced the idea! I did not realise that these experiences were there to show me another way, until much later.

Occasionally I would be asked to run the knee group. I loved this; I would set up and join in the class, moving around, encouraging, correcting, and trying to get some group momentum. Then I would set up a therapy couch screened off, and everyone had at least 5 minutes of stretching measuring, needles, taping, or touch base time. It was intense, but I was there to do my best, or at least I thought so. I was just being myself; I was not trying to show my colleague up. I was running the class according to how I was taught and what would be the best way to make sure everyone had some personal attention. Within two weeks, we had full attendance and full enthused participation. This caused problems (of course). It's funny now, but as a culture, we don't tend to protest or kick up a fuss, so for these patients to go on strike and refuse to come to class unless I was running it, was quite assertive. Of course, that did not happen, and of course, that junior member didn't ask what I did differently, I just got into trouble! Thankfully this incident did not deter me from championing patients, it just made me very aware that there are different kinds of therapists, and it cemented for me the kind of Physiotherapist I wanted to be.

Another time I got hauled into the office, apparently, I was taking too long to discharge patients, and one particular lady had been on my list for a year, which, according to my boss, meant she was depriving someone else. I explained my reasons. The consultant had said he was not prepared to operate on her, she was too overweight, the medication the GP put her on was causing her to gain weight, and she couldn't exercise as her knee was so painful, in addition, she wasn't sleeping. She did not know how to break the cycle. I gave her a course of acupuncture with the appropriate rehab and then progressed her to a self-care package. I would, between patients, needle her, or she would come in and start her programme, and I would needle her after. Either way, she did not have her own time slot. In the end, wasn't I saving the NHS money? She did not need to see the GP; take costly, ineffective medication, and she was motivated to be strong and well. I just did not understand this idea of separate budgets and limited time. These people were the very people we were enlisted to help. Yet ridiculous outmoded ideas and practices were the norm, and none of them are put in place to help the people that we trained to help.

Another critical moment for me evolving on purpose was finding out I was pregnant. Life threw another opportunity to heal some childhood wounds. It was both delightful and daunting in equal measure and nothing short of miraculous. I had my left ovary and fallopian tube removed six months previously due to a benign tumour on my ovary. My right ovary had folded over and stuck to my abdominal wall. I had so many questions and doubts, would this baby be born? Would I be an awful Mother? Maybe I would have violent rages. How would I know what to do? Babies are easy, but what about guidance, boundaries, helping that little person understand their place in the world. Work, in the NHS instead of being understanding and supportive, was awful. My boss demanded that I prove I was HIV negative, colleagues making snide remarks about did I know who the father was. Sometimes my work schedule was so busy I would faint from exhaustion, and my boss would give me a telling-off in front of everyone "You are pregnant, you don't have a disease, you can have a ten-minute break and no more. You can't eat at your desk either"; great no time for a drink, unable to have a snack. My private work in a local practice also took advantage, they underpaid me by a significant amount.

This daily haranguing and the constant threat of withdrawing my permission to work privately had me stressed and tearful. I was worried about my unborn child, concerned about finances, and some days I just felt plain overwhelmed and exhausted. The only thing I could do was put one foot in front of the other and take each day at a time. There were people who witnessed what was happening; the receptionist would put "fake patients" in my diary, or pre-booked sessions were not rubbed out when the person was discharged. That helped me immensely. Another person gave me some sound human resources advice and told me my rights. I snapped out of feeling like a victim. A turning point: I felt empowered, had choices, and did not have to stick it out for more than another week! I felt jubilant. I left at 28 weeks and started working privately. I had more work offered than hours in the day, which boosted my confidence and bank balance. I also had plenty of new contacts and places to work. Despite some horrendous times, my work brought me joy; patients collectively looked after me, bringing me food and little gifts before and after my daughter was born.

Motherhood really supported my emotional growth; I had to face certain demons and look at my values and what kind of parent I wanted to be. My parents, of course, did the best they could with the resources they had and some values I believed to be good ones, so I kept them; other ideas were less so. I am pleased to report that my daughter is 19 and I have just waved her off to Uni. She is bold, passionate about positive social policy, hates injustice, is quite the nurturer of others but does not stand for any BS. To say that I am proud of her is an understatement—anyhow, back to me!

I have always wondered why the pursuit of scientific evidence is deemed a hallowed pursuit and is the "only truth" In 2009 when The National Institute of Clinical Excellence reviewed acupuncture as a pain-relieving modality, a Professor at UCH, University College Hospital in London, described it as the dark arts! The older I get, and the more I read about both, I see that the lines are perhaps a lot less distinct. As a human, our experiences aren't just about how our cells are sending messages (and vice versa), or the structures and tissues at fault, but an integration between mind, body and our deeper conscious self. Why does one person experience symptoms in one way and not another? It has been well documented that Fibromyalgia, for example, is strongly connected with trauma, whether it is physical or emotional. Chronic pain often has its roots in trauma and causes the maladaptation of the Central Nervous System. Is it possible or probable that there is a deeper part of ourselves that is also in distress? How can staying in a job that demeans you, an abusive relationship or marriage, or a dangerous neighbourhood with no outside space not have a detrimental effect on our finely tuned systems? For example, the Amygdala, which is part of the limbic system, and monitors perceived threats, is closely connected with our response to trauma. This becomes overactive and overprotective and enlarges, to the point where it is bigger than the prefrontal cortex, our higher function/thinking part of the brain. Many studies show that this actually shrinks and loses networks. When this happens, we are biologically operating on a survival perspective and therefore our decisions are made based on this. Leaders in the field of pain and trauma (e.g Peter Levine, Lorimer Mosely and Bessel A Van der Kolk) have all demonstrated the brain's ability to rewire itself; enabling us to rid ourselves of behaviour patterns, thoughts and trauma responses. Unfortunately (or fortunately) these processes require time, deep commitment and a tenacity that we don't all possess. Furthermore, outcomes are variable, as we all are. Therefore science and scientific methodology tend to reject it.

It has also been demonstrated that sound waves set at specific frequencies (Solfeggio) and meditation, to name a few, can also reverse some of these brain changes. These are not new methods, they have been around for hundreds (if not thousands) of years. The best part of these therapies is that they adapt to your requirements. On the other hand, pharmaceuticals will never achieve that level of adaptability. Yet, so much money is made, invested and wasted in this pursuit. Perhaps science does not hold all the answers?

Over 30 years ago, I was introduced to the action potential in a lab in a central London university. I was irritated beyond belief. What the hell did any of this have to do with Physiotherapy? Thirty years later, this incredible unit of electricity holds such fascination for me, oh the irony! So excited by the depth of this oh so taken for granted electrical signal produced by so many in the cells in the body. I sat up one night, totally overcome with excitement. Something stirred deep within me, my brain was whirring with what this might mean - this electrical unit holds the key. Because of its properties, it can be measured both in health and illness, thereby qualifying it for scientific method. Yet simultaneously, the action potential (or electrical unit) surely is related to signals we emit (i.e. our "vibe"). For example, the heart muscle has its own specific channels that produce electrical impulses, our heartbeat. We absolutely know that these units fire to warn the brain that pain is incoming and these firing sequences become disrupted. For example, the threshold that causes them to fire becomes lowered long term. Ectopic firing also occurs, whereby no painful stimulus is present but these units keep firing to warn the brain of a non-existent problem. Studies inform us that the useful protective function of pain becomes massively exaggerated and is perceived as a safety threat, hence the changes that were described earlier. This is chronic pain.

In chronic pain, which is my area of interest and where much of my clinical expertise lies, I like to know why, how does this fit together, what are we missing? How does this translate into helping patients? I found some answers in the form of Frequency Specific Microcurrent (FSM). Healthy performing muscles, nerves, joints, and organs have been calibrated to emit certain frequencies, much like the string of a violin which, when struck, will resonate with and cause the string of another violin to start producing sound as long as there is no interference. FSM can help to re-establish the frequency your systems should be emitting. Don't quote me on this—I am not writing a physics paper here! I have been using this for several months now and getting some very good results. I will be writing a proposal to incorporate a trial for the final part of my MSc. I would like to believe that all my life experiences, from my birth until now, have led me through an interesting and winding path to reach a place of passion about those suffering with chronic pain. I haven't got all the answers, but I hope I can help you, to tap into your own source of healing and wellbeing. I know you can, you just need to give yourself permission.

In a nutshell, there is a mismatch between the information being inputted from the outside world and our internal processing of this information. It is the processing in our internal environment that is the problem. We cannot control the external input, but we have some control over our processes within our internal environment.

In the meantime, I am running low-cost pain relief clinics using FSM, electro-acupuncture, TENS, and some other modalities. Maybe I will meet some of you there. Expect to hear sound healing in the background and wafts of exotic oils, all deliberately designed to soothe your senses.

ABOUT THE AUTHOR
TRACEY KISSOON

Tracey lives in the Cotswolds where she has her own thriving physiotherapy practice. She combines her love of biomechanics and muscle imbalance with Chinese medicine, reflexology, and intuition. She is currently finishing her MSc at Keele University and is excited to combine her newly acquired knowledge and experience in pain physiology to support her clients even more. When she is not swotting for a deadline, she can be found tending her scruffy but sacred allotment where miracles unfold on a daily basis; as well as cooking or making flavoured gins with some of her produce.

Website: www.physiokinesis.co.uk.

20

ABOUT THE PUBLISHER
SOULFUL VALLEY PUBLISHING

Katie Carey founded the Soulful Valley Publishing House on the 4th of May 2021, spiritually a significant date in her family. Katie heard the call from spirit to create a publishing house following her collaboration in a multi-author book called "Intuitive: Knowing Her Truth", where she became an International Best-Selling Author.

Katie channelled her first few book titles and knew that those titles were important to bring into creation.

Katie is the podcast host of the Soulfulvalley global ranked in the Top 2% of listened too podcasts. She uses both the podcast and the multi-author books as a platform to help metaphysical coaches and energy healers to elevate their work so that the people they are here to serve can find them.

Katie was the founder of STAGES a charity she ran for 7 years supporting people with Mental Health conditions and their families with Mindfulness and Alternative Therapies, where she won the Educational Spirit of Corby Award in 2017.

Katie studied psychology and the science of the mind in mental health as part of her degree to help her understand the science behind our minds whilst leading the charity, alongside psychic development and mediumship training.

Katie loves blending science and spirituality together and has attracted people with the same mindset, into her first multi-author book. Most have stories of synchronicities that led to them writing in the book with Katie.

Katie's aim is to bring these concepts and ideas to more people who are seeking ways to support their own mental, spiritual, emotional, and physical wellbeing.

Katie has a history of working in TV, Radio and Theatre as an Actress and Singer, which she manifested into her life in her teens.

Katie lives in a Northamptonshire Village in the UK and is a Mum to 3 Adult children and Nanna to her grandchildren and intends to make it her life's work to educate people into finding healthier solutions and breaking ancestral and generational patterns of lack and trauma. Katie is passionate about raising consciousness and currently does this with her work as a Mentor/Coach, Podcaster, Publisher and through her songs and poetry.

If you would like to collaborate with Katie in one of her multi-author books or you would like to write your own solo book, you can contact Katie:

Website: www.soulfulvalley.com
Email: soulfulvalleypodcast@gmail.com
FB, Twitter, IG and LinkedIn @soulfulvalley

Made in the USA
Las Vegas, NV
19 November 2021